McGraw-Hill Ryerson

*Math*Links 8

PRACTICE AND HOMEWORK BOOK

Authors

Victor Epp
Hon. B.A., M.Ed.
School District 5
(Southeast Kootenay)
British Columbia

Tricia Licorish (Perry)
B.Ed.
St. James-Assiniboia
School Division
Manitoba

Get Ready Authors

Bruce McAskill
B.Sc., B.Ed., M.Ed., Ph.D.
Mathematics Consultant
Victoria, British Columbia

Wayne Watt
B.Sc., B.Ed., M.Ed.
Mathematics Consultant
Winnipeg, Manitoba

Stella Ablett
B.Sc., B.Ed., M.Ed.
Mulgrave School, West
Vancouver (Independent)
British Columbia

Blaise Johnson
B.Sc., B.Ed.
School District 45
(West Vancouver)
British Columbia

Greg McInulty
B.Sc., B.Ed.
Edmonton Public Schools
Alberta

Michael Webb
B.Sc., M.Sc., Ph.D.
Mathematics Consultant
Toronto, Ontario

Rick Wunderlich
B.Ed.
School District 83 (North
Okanagan/Shuswap)
British Columbia

Chris Zarski
B.Ed., M.Ed.
Evergreen Catholic Separate
Regional Division No. 2
Alberta

Developmental Team

Joanne Aldridge
Edmonton Public Schools
Alberta

Ted Keating
Thompson Rivers University
British Columbia

Cheryl Makokis
Edmonton Public Schools
Alberta

Ian Strachan
Calgary Board of Education
Alberta

Robert Wong
Edmonton Public Schools
Alberta

McGraw-Hill Ryerson

Toronto   Montréal   Boston   Burr Ridge, IL   Dubuque, IA   Madison, WI   New York
San Francisco   St. Louis   Bangkok   Bogotá   Caracas   Kuala Lumpur   Lisbon   London
Madrid   Mexico City   Milan   New Delhi   Santiago   Seoul   Singapore   Sydney   Taipei

The McGraw·Hill Companies

McGraw-Hill
Ryerson

COPIES OF THIS BOOK
MAY BE OBTAINED BY
CONTACTING:

McGraw-Hill Ryerson Ltd.

WEB SITE:
http://www.mcgrawhill.ca

E-MAIL:
orders@mcgrawhill.ca

TOLL-FREE FAX:
1-800-463-5885

TOLL-FREE CALL:
1-800-565-5758

OR BY MAILING YOUR
ORDER TO:
McGraw-Hill Ryerson
Order Department
300 Water Street
Whitby, ON L1N 9B6

Please quote the ISBN
and title when placing
your order.

Student text
ISBN: 0-07-097-338-5

Practice and
Homework Book
ISBN: 978-0-07-07097342-8

McGraw-Hill Ryerson
MathLinks 8 Practice and Homework Book

ISBN-13: 978-0-07-07097342-8
ISBN-10: 0-07-097342-3

http://www.mcgrawhill.ca

3 4 5 6 7 8 9 10   MP   1 9 8 7 6 5 4 3 2

Printed and bound in Canada

PUBLISHER: Linda Allison
PROJECT MANAGER: Helen Mason
CONTENT MANAGER: Jean Ford
DEVELOPMENTAL EDITORS: Ann Firth, Adrienne Montgomerie
MANAGER, EDITORIAL SERVICES: Crystal Shortt
SUPERVISING EDITORS: Shannon Martin, Jaime Smith
COPY EDITOR: Linda Jenkins, Red Pen Services
EDITORIAL ASSISTANT: Erin Hartley
MANAGER, PRODUCTION SERVICES: Yolanda Pigden
SENIOR PRODUCTION CO-ORDINATOR: Paula Brown
COVER DESIGN: Valid Design & Layout
ELECTRONIC PAGE MAKE-UP: aptara, The Content Transformation Company

Contents

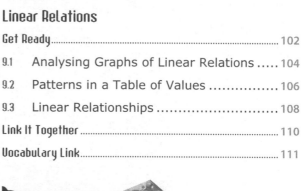

To the User

Welcome to the *MathLinks 8* Practice and Homework Book. This print resource provides additional opportunities for you to develop the skills you used in the *MathLinks 8* student resource.

- Each chapter begins with a Get Ready that can be used to help you reinforce the skills you will need to be successful with that chapter.
- The chapter content is divided into sections. Each section starts with a review of the Key Ideas. This is followed by a series of questions that allow you to practise and apply the skills and concepts from that section in the *MathLinks 8* student resource.
- The end of each chapter includes a Link It Together page that challenges you to combine the skills and concepts you learned during the chapter to solve problems.
- The final page of each chapter is a Vocabulary Link that reviews the key words and other important words from each chapter in the form of a word puzzle of some kind.
- There are pages of centimetre grid paper, 0.5 centimetre grid paper, and isometric dot paper starting on page 146 if you wish to make larger graphs and sketches.
- Answers for all questions appear at the end of the practice and homework book starting on page 152.

Additional activities, as well as games and puzzles, are available in McGraw-Hill Ryerson's Online Learning Centre. Go to **www.mathlinks8.ca** and follow the links to the Student Centre or to the Parent Centre. The Parent Centre also includes suggestions for helping your child in mathematics.

Authors
MathLinks 8 Practice and Homework Book

Bar Graphs and Double Bar Graphs

The **bar graph** shows that Zoe has twice as many science fiction books as books about sports.

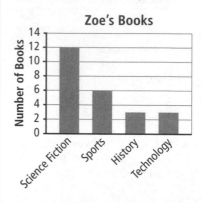

Zoe's Books

The **double bar graph** shows that Matt has twice as many sports books as Zoe has.

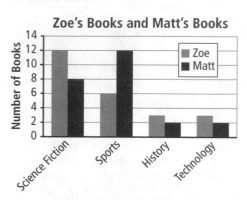

Zoe's Books and Matt's Books

The bars in bar graphs can be vertical or horizontal. Bar graphs leave space between each data category.

1. Use the bar graph about Zoe's books to answer the question: If the bars were drawn horizontally, what would change on the graph? What would stay the same? Redraw the bar graph using horizontal bars.

2. Use the double bar graph to answer these questions.

   a) How many more sports books does Matt have than history books?

   b) Write another question you could ask about the graph. Develop an answer for your question.

Circle Graphs

The **circle graph** shows the different activities that Akira does online.

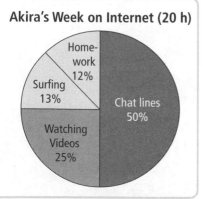

Akira's Week on Internet (20 h)

3. Use the circle graph to answer these questions.

a) What activity did Akira spend the most time on? How many hours did she spend?

b) Would this circle graph make sense if the titles or labels were missing? Explain.

Line Graphs

The **line graph** shows changes in average maximum temperature for each month in Whitehorse, Yukon Territory.

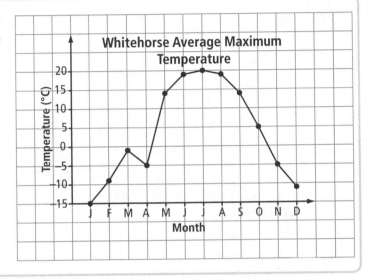

4. Use the line graph to answer these questions.

a) When did the greatest temperature change happen?

b) Do you think the trend of rising and falling temperatures will continue? Explain.

Pictographs

The **pictograph** shows that more T-shirts were sold on Thursday than on any other day that week.

5. Use the pictograph to answer these questions.

a) How many more T-shirts were sold on Thursday than on Friday?

b) Explain how you used the pictograph to answer part a).

1.1 Advantages and Disadvantages of Different Graphs

MathLinks 8, pages 6–17

Key Ideas Review

Column B lists several types of graphs. Write the type of graph from column B that best matches the description in column A.

A	B
1. _____ are best for comparing categories to the whole using percents.	**a)** Bar graphs
2. _____ are best for showing changes in data over time.	**b)** Line graphs
3. _____ are best for comparing two sets of data across categories.	**c)** Pictographs
4. _____ are best for comparing data that can be easily counted and represented using symbols.	**d)** Circle graphs
5. _____ are best for comparing data across categories.	**e)** Double bar graphs

Practise and Apply

6. The student council recorded the number of grade 7, 8, and 9 students who attended the spring dance.

Spring Dance Attendance (300 students)

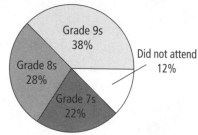

- Grade 9s 38%
- Did not attend 12%
- Grade 8s 28%
- Grade 7s 22%

Spring Dance Attendance

Grade 7s ⊙⊙⊙⊙⊙⊙(
Grade 8s ⊙⊙⊙⊙⊙⊙⊙
Grade 9s ⊙⊙⊙⊙⊙⊙⊙⊙⊙(
Did not attend ⊙⊙⊙

⊙ Represents 12 students

a) How many more grade 9 students attended the dance compared to the number of grade 8 students? Which graph shows this more clearly? Explain.

b) Which graph better shows the number of students who did not attend the dance? Justify your answer.

c) Describe one advantage of using each graph.

7. The graphs show the popularity of healthy food choices, such as mixes of nuts and dried fruit, sold in a school vending machine during the first three months of school.

Healthy Food Choices

a) How many more healthy items were sold in November compared to sales in September? Which graph displays this more clearly? Explain your answer.

b) Between which two months was the greatest increase in sales of healthy items?

c) Describe one disadvantage of using each graph.

8. These tables show the points scored during the first five games of the girls' basketball season.

Lindsay		Jo-Anna	
Game	Points	Game	Points
1	18	1	10
2	22	2	12
3	16	3	8
4	20	4	22
5	30	5	20

a) Draw a double bar graph and a double line graph to display these data.

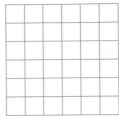

b) Compare the two graphs you drew. Does one present the data more clearly? Explain your answer.

9. The table shows the number of games Leah sold at the Village Games Shop in July.

Type of Game	Number Sold
Puzzle	7
Board	13
Computer	10
Video	5

a) Choose one type of graph to display these data. Explain your choice.

b) Would a line graph be a good choice to display these data? Justify your answer.

1.2 Misrepresenting Data

MathLinks 8, pages 18–27

Key Ideas Review

Choose from the following terms to complete #1.

data	false	scale	visuals

1. a) People may misinterpret _____ and draw _____ conclusions when graphs are misleading.

b) Misleading features of graphs may include the following:

- Distorting the _____.

- Distorting the information by using _____ of different sizes.

Practise and Apply

2. Three employees' sales for one week are shown in the following graph.

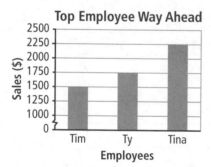

Top Employee Way Ahead

a) Explain how this graph could be misleading.

b) How much more did Tina sell compared to Ty?

c) How should the graph be drawn to make it clearer?

3. A tropical destination wants to increase the number of travellers to its resort. The marketing director is trying to decide which graph about rainfall should be included in the new brochure.

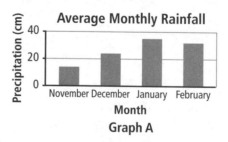

Graph A

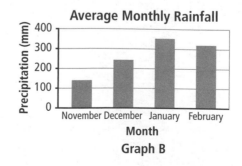

Graph B

a) How are the two graphs different?

b) Explain how Graph A could be misleading.

c) Which graph do you think the director should choose? Explain your answer.

4. The fans at a football game were asked which team they were supporting. This graph shows the results of the survey.

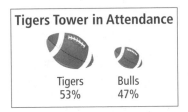

Tigers Tower in Attendance

Tigers 53%   Bulls 47%

a) Which team had more supporters at the game, and by how much?

b) How is this graph misleading?

c) How could you draw a graph to show the data more accurately?

5. Jaime and Ashton are training for the marathon. The graph below shows how many kilometres they have completed in their training so far.

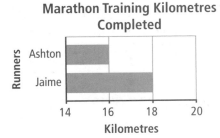

Marathon Training Kilometres Completed

a) How many more kilometres has Jaime completed?

b) Describe how to redraw the graph to represent the data more accurately.

6. The information below shows Keisha's practice times for band. She wants to make her practice times look better than they are. Draw the graph she might create. Explain how your graph distorts the data.

Week	1	2	3	4
Practice Time (minutes)	40	25	30	10

1.3 Critiquing Data Presentation

MathLinks 8, pages 28–35

Key Ideas Review

There are several important factors to consider when critiquing a graph. Write the factor from column B that best matches the analysis question in column A.

A	B
1. Consider the graph _____ when determining whether the graph is informative.	a) type
2. Consider the graph _____ when determining whether the graph is designed in a way that represents the data accurately.	b) format
3. Consider the graph _____ when determining whether the graph is the best choice for the data.	c) usefulness

Practise and Apply

4. Milo is writing to ask the school board to change the snacks in the school vending machines. Before writing the letter, he completes a survey of the snack foods students prefer and displays the results in the graph below.

Popular Snacks

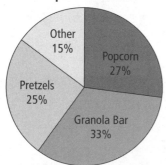

a) Why do you think Milo used a circle graph to display the data?

b) Does this graph argue his point to change the snacks in the vending machine?

5. The following graph shows activities participated in at two different recreational parks.

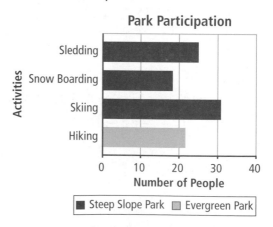

a) What conclusions can you make about the graph?

b) Is this graph the best choice for the data? Explain.

c) Using the graph that you did not choose for part b), what could this graph be used to describe?

6. Zach and Jessie must pick a summer job. They have narrowed their options down to two choices. Each one makes a graph.

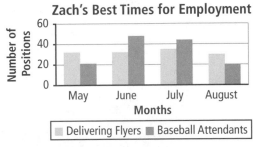
Zach's Best Times for Employment

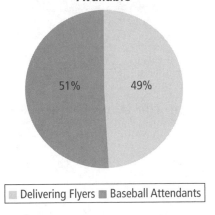
Jessie's Summer Employment Available

Delivering Flyers ■ Baseball Attendants

a) What information does each graph show?

b) Which graph best displays the information Zach and Jessie need to make a decision? Explain.

7. Stephanie recorded how many times she chose to do each activity in one week to make a favourite activity list.

Which Activity?

a) What does this graph show about Stephanie's interests?

b) What conclusion could be drawn from this graph?

Link It Together

Matt and Anu are doing a science experiment where they make their own toothpaste. They survey their peers to find the most popular flavours of toothpaste.

Toothpaste Flavours	Votes
Peppermint	12
Mint	8
Bubblegum	15

1. **a)** Which type of graph provides the best way to display the data? Justify your choice.

   b) Draw the graph you have chosen.

   c) Name one advantage and one disadvantage of using the type of graph you chose.

2. **a)** Peppermint is the easiest flavour to add to toothpaste. Create a graph that is misleading to show that peppermint is just as popular as bubblegum. Explain.

   b) Is any other type of graph just as informative, or more informative than the one you chose? Explain.

Vocabulary Link

Unscramble the letters of each term. The terms are one to three words long. Use the clues to help you solve the puzzles.

A	B
1. Zoe's Books and Matt's Books	RABGPLEHBOUDRA
2. Zoe's Books	ARHGPABR
3. general direction in which a line graph is going	DETNR
4. Whitehorse Average Maximum Temperature	RAEPIHNLG
5. change the appearance or twist the meaning of something in a way that is misleading	SDITOTR
6. Akira's Week on Internet (20 h)	RCPIACREHLG
7. T-Shirts Sales	PPAOCGTHRI
8. spread between the smallest and largest numbers in a range of numbers	ALNRVTEI
9. Population Trends	BPHEIDAUNEOLRLG

Writing Ratios

A **ratio** is a comparison of quantities that have the same units. The order of the words in a sentence indicates the order of the numbers in the ratio. Ratios can be written in several ways.

The ratio of black balls to the total number of balls can be expressed using
- *Words*: three compared to nine or 3 to 9
- *Ratio Notation*: $3:9$
- *Fractions*: $\frac{3}{9}$

1. For the diagram shown above, write each ratio. Express each answer three different ways.

   a) black balls to white balls

   b) white balls to total balls

2. For the diagram shown above, what does each of the following ratios represent?

   a) $6:3$

   b) $3:9$

Equivalent Fractions

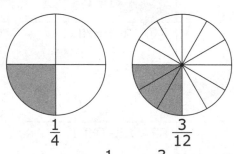

$$\frac{1}{4} \qquad \frac{3}{12}$$

The fractions $\frac{1}{4}$ and $\frac{3}{12}$ are **equivalent fractions.** They are different names for the same fraction.

Two fractions are equivalent if you can multiply or divide the numerator and denominator of one fraction by the same number to get the second fraction.

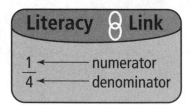

Literacy Link

$$\frac{1 \leftarrow \text{numerator}}{4 \leftarrow \text{denominator}}$$

$$\begin{array}{c} \times 3 \\ \frac{1}{4} = \frac{3}{12} \\ \times 3 \end{array} \qquad \begin{array}{c} \div 3 \\ \frac{3}{12} = \frac{1}{4} \\ \div 3 \end{array}$$

3. Are the following fractions equivalent? Show how you know.

a) $\frac{2}{3}$ and $\frac{6}{9}$ b) $\frac{1}{5}$ and $\frac{4}{20}$

4. List two equivalent fractions for each of the following.

a) $\frac{1}{4}$ b) $\frac{4}{12}$

5. Identify the missing value to make an equivalent fraction. Show how you calculated each value.

a) $\frac{5}{8} = \frac{\boxed{}}{24}$

b) $\frac{1}{3} = \frac{5}{\boxed{}}$

Comparing Quantities

A fraction can represent part of a whole. One half of the rectangle is shaded.

The top line is $\frac{2}{5}$, $\frac{10}{25}$, or $\frac{20}{50}$ of the bottom line.

Think of the number line labelled as $\frac{2}{5}$.

Think of the number line labelled as $\frac{10}{25}$.

How could you label a number line to represent $\frac{20}{50}$?

You can use a **multiplier** to compare two quantities. In the diagram, Line 2 is 4 times as long as Line 1.

The multiplier of Line 2 compared to Line 1 is 4, or the ratio $\frac{4}{1}$.

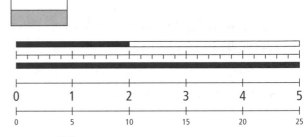

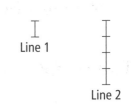

Line 1

Line 2

6. Give three equivalent fractions that compare the top line to the bottom line.

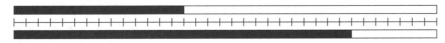

7. What is the multiplier from Figure 1 to Figure 2?

a)

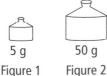

5 g   50 g

Figure 1   Figure 2

b)   12 mm   36 mm

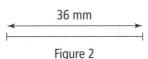

Figure 1   Figure 2

2.1 Two-Term and Three-Term Ratios

MathLinks 8, pages 46–54

Key Ideas Review

1. Decide whether each of the following statements is true or false. Circle the word
    True or *False*. If the statement is false, rewrite it to make it true.

    a) **True**/**False** A part-to-part ratio compares different parts of several groups.

    _____

    _____

    b) **True**/**False** A part-to-whole ratio compares one part of a group to the
       whole group.

    _____

    _____

    c) **True**/**False** A part-to-part ratio can be written as a fraction,
       decimal, or percent. For example, the ratio of flowers to leaves

       is $\dfrac{\boxed{}}{12}$ or $\dfrac{\boxed{}}{3}$, _____, or _____%.

    _____

    _____

    d) **True**/**False** A three-term ratio compares three quantities
       measured in the same units.

    _____

    _____

    e) **True**/**False** A two-term ratio compares two quantities measured in the
       same scale.

    _____

    _____

Practise and Apply

2. Write each ratio using ratio notation.
    Then, write the ratios in lowest terms.

    a) Three red tiles compared to nine
       black tiles.

    b) In a hotel, 23 rooms have a double
       bed and 9 have a queen-size bed.
       What is the ratio of double beds to
       queen-size beds to total beds?

c) A bike rack contains 5 road bikes and 15 mountain bikes.

d) Over two weeks, eight days were cloudy and six were sunny.

e) The arena schedule lists 10 hockey games, 8 skating classes, and 2 family times. Compare hockey games to total time slots.

f) The room has 16 chairs and 4 tables. Compare chairs to pieces of furniture.

3. Fill in the missing number to make each fraction equivalent.

a) $\frac{1}{3} = \frac{\boxed{}}{6}$ **b)** $\frac{\boxed{}}{3} = \frac{10}{15}$

c) $\frac{5}{6} = \frac{\boxed{}}{12}$ **d)** $\frac{40}{50} = \frac{80}{\boxed{}}$

4. There are 9 black tiles to 3 white tiles.

a) Draw the ratio.

b) Write the part-to-part ratio that corresponds with the drawing.

c) Write two part-to-whole ratios that correspond with the drawing.

d) Write the ratios in part c) as equivalent fractions in lowest terms.

5. What part(s) of this diagram could be represented by each of the following ratios?

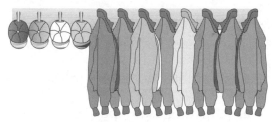

a) 1 to 2

b) $8 : 12 : 4$

c) $3 : 2$

d) $\frac{12}{24}$

6. In a class of 28 students, 20 took band and the rest took choir. Use ratio notation to answer the following.

a) What is the ratio of choir members to total students in the class?

b) What is the ratio of band members to choir members?

7. A mixed cereal contains 150 g of rice, 300 g of wheat, and 400 g of oats. Write the ratio in decimal form to compare the types of grains in the cereal. Show your thinking and round the decimals to the nearest hundredth.

2.2 Rates

MathLinks 8, pages 55–62

Key Ideas Review

1. Unscramble the letters to form a word in each blank to complete the statement.

   a) A rate is a comparison of two quantities measured in _____
   TFDIFEERN
   units.

   b) A rate can be expressed as a _____, but cannot be
   OFNARTCI
   expressed as a _____.
   REPTCNE

   c) A unit rate is a rate in which the second term is _____.
   NOE

   d) To compare the cost of similar items a unit _____ is useful.
   EPCIR

Practise and Apply

2. Determine the unit rate. Show your thinking.

   a) Riding 50 km in 3 h. Round your answer to the nearest hundredth.

   b) Typing 660 words in 10 minutes.

   c) Moving 216 students in 4 buses.

   d) Carrying 138 apples in 6 bags.

   e) Raising $315 in 35 h.

   f) Driving 220 km in $2\frac{1}{2}$ h.

3. Calculate the unit rate for each situation. Show your thinking. Then, circle the greater rate for each pair.

   a) $210 for 30 h or $198 for 20 h

   b) 574 km in 7 h or 420 km in 5 h

   c) 64 h of sunlight in 16 days or 69 h sunlight in 23 days

4. The Mitchells' car used half a tank of gas when travelling from Edmonton to Calgary, a trip of about 300 km. If the fuel tank's capacity is 54 L, what was the car's fuel consumption rate in L/100 km?

5. You are shopping for yogurt.

a) What is the unit price for each container of yogurt?

b) What is the unit price per 100 g for each container of yogurt?

c) Which container is the best buy? Explain your thinking.

_____

_____

_____

6. Jeremy earned $1365 after working for half of a year. He expects to continue working for the same number of hours each month, at the same pay rate.

a) How much will he earn in total after working for a year? Show two different ways of arriving at the answer.

_____

_____

b) If he works 10 hours a week, what is his hourly rate of pay? Show your thinking.

_____

_____

7. This table lists the approximate area and population of five countries.

Country	Population	Land Area (km²)	Density
Canada	31 006 000	9 220 000	
Ecuador	12 562 000	278 000	
France	58 978 000	546 000	
Netherlands	15 808 000	34 000	
United States	272 640 000	9 159 000	

a) Calculate the population density (population/km²) for each country listed. Show your thinking below, then record the values in the table rounded to the nearest hundredth.

b) List the countries in order from greatest density to least density.

_____

_____

_____

_____

_____

c) Is population density a rate? **Yes No** Explain.

_____

_____

2.3 Proportional Reasoning

MathLinks 8, pages 63–69

Key Ideas Review

Choose from the following terms to complete #1 and #2.

equal	proportion	ratios	unit rate

1. A proportion is a relationship that says that two _____ or rates

   are _____.

2. Identify the method shown in each example, then solve for the missing value.

   a) Using a _____.

   $$\frac{\$6}{4 \text{ advocadoes}} \xrightarrow{\times 2.5} \frac{\$\boxed{}}{10 \text{ advocadoes}}$$

   Missing value is $6 × 2.5 = $_____

   b) Using a _____.

   $$\frac{\$6}{4 \text{ advocados}} = \frac{\$1.50}{1 \text{ advocado}}$$

   $10 × \$1.50 = \$$_____

Practise and Apply

3. Determine the unit rate. Show your thinking.

   a) Riding a bicycle 50 km in 2 h.

   b) A pack of 10 pencils for $2.49.

   Pencil $ 2.49

   c) Running 400 m in 80 s.

   d) Ground beef costs $5.99 for 3 kg.

4. Fill in the missing value. Show your thinking.

   a) $\dfrac{1}{4} = \dfrac{\boxed{}}{12}$

   b) $\dfrac{12}{16} = \dfrac{\boxed{}}{4}$

   c) $\dfrac{10}{\boxed{}} = \dfrac{2}{5}$

   d) $\dfrac{\boxed{}}{21} = \dfrac{4}{7}$

5. Determine the missing value to make each rate equivalent. Include the units.

   a) $\dfrac{16 \text{ roses}}{2 \text{ bouquets}} = \dfrac{\boxed{} \text{ roses}}{1 \text{ bouquet}}$

   b) $\dfrac{190 \text{ km}}{2 \text{ h}} = \dfrac{\boxed{} \text{ km}}{8 \text{ h}}$

6. Set up a proportion for each situation.

   a) A plant that is 40 cm tall has a planter that is 20 cm wide. If it grows to a height of 50 cm, it will need a planter 25 cm wide.

   b) If there are 60 mL of sugar in 600 mL of pop, then 1 L of pop contains 100 mL of sugar.

   c) A car needs 9.4 L of gasoline to go 100 km. It will need 56.4 L to go 600 km.

7. There are 42 players on 7 volleyball teams. How many players are on 4 teams? Show your thinking.

8. Trevor is a high school quarterback. On average, out of each 16 attempts, he completes 5 out of 8 passes and throws 1 pass that is intercepted. Set up a proportion to answer each question, and then write a sentence answer.

   a) If Trevor passes 40 times, how many completions would he be expected to make?

   b) In last week's game, he attempted 32 passes. How many were likely intercepted?

9. Fill in the missing value in each equivalent fraction. Show your thinking.

   a) $\dfrac{\boxed{}}{20} = \dfrac{4}{5} = \dfrac{\boxed{}}{30}$

   b) $\dfrac{\$4.14}{3\ kg} = \dfrac{\boxed{}}{1\ kg} = \dfrac{\boxed{}}{7\ kg}$

10. Car A used 40.5 L of gasoline to travel 450 km. Car B used 18.7 L to travel 220 km. Circle the car with better fuel mileage. Justify your answer by calculating each car's L/100 km rate. Show your work.

11. On a map of Alberta, Edson is 2 cm from Spruce Grove. A proportion on the map shows that 3 cm on the map equals 225 km on the ground. Write the correct distance on the highway sign. Show your thinking.

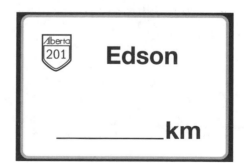

Link It Together

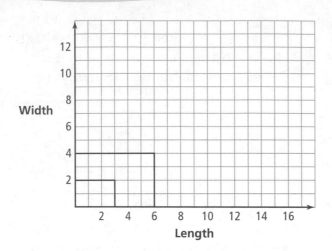

1. **a)** Write a ratio for the two rectangles on the graph.

   b) On the graph, draw the next three rectangles that continue the pattern.

   c) Complete the table. Show your thinking.

Rectangle	Length	Width	Area (square units)	Area Difference (square units)
P	3	2	6	—
Q	6	4	24	18
R	9		54	30
S				
T				

   d) Write the width to the length ratio of these rectangles as a fraction in lowest terms.

   d) Predict the area of rectangle U. Show your thinking.

Vocabulary Link

Draw a line from the example in column A to the correct term in column B, and then find each term in the word search. Note that the words in the word search do not have any hyphens.

A	B
1. $\times\ 170$ $\dfrac{3 \text{ plants}}{0.5 \text{ m}^2} = \dfrac{\boxed{}}{85 \text{ m}^2}$ $\times\ 170$	**a)** part-to-part ratio **b)** part-to-whole ratio **c)** proportion **d)** rate **e)** three-term ratio **f)** two-term ratio **g)** unit price **h)** unit rate
2. 12 km/h	
3. 33¢/1	
4. three red balloons in a drawer to four blue balloons in a drawer	
5. 3 red balloons in a drawer to 16 balloons in a drawer	
6. 2 : 3	
7. 3 : 4 : 6	
8. 45 km in 3 h	

```
E  I  D  M  Z  B  Z  I  C  D  X  G  L  F  K  F  S  J  B  F
C  Y  K  T  Y  L  G  J  R  P  Z  B  E  X  J  J  D  B  Y  T
W  V  J  H  Z  G  U  I  C  A  M  F  D  H  W  O  Y  V  D  J
V  L  X  R  N  X  J  W  A  R  F  S  C  U  F  X  C  C  S  T
P  A  U  E  B  X  T  G  R  T  I  L  P  Y  T  P  Z  H  G  K
F  F  X  E  V  N  R  I  S  T  X  G  T  O  U  R  D  P  C  G
D  P  X  T  S  O  X  U  J  O  E  X  I  Q  J  O  Q  W  T  Q
T  U  U  E  X  V  L  H  M  P  Q  T  C  C  I  P  E  I  G  B
S  N  N  R  O  X  T  E  K  A  A  J  M  X  Q  O  N  W  B  U
I  I  I  M  Z  A  R  Q  E  R  K  C  T  B  G  R  E  M  M  L
I  T  T  R  F  L  I  M  M  T  W  F  F  Z  U  T  S  M  H  K
U  R  P  A  E  V  Y  R  A  R  L  H  D  E  V  I  N  J  J  P
G  A  R  T  S  L  E  K  P  A  K  T  R  X  C  O  M  A  P  J
G  T  I  I  F  T  F  T  M  T  L  B  Z  A  L  N  L  V  I  M
X  E  C  O  O  E  A  M  S  I  O  X  H  R  T  D  K  F  M  W
F  Y  E  W  N  N  J  L  C  O  M  P  Q  O  G  E  C  T  D  A
B  D  T  P  A  R  T  T  O  W  H  O  L  E  R  A  T  I  O  S
L  B  X  J  Z  I  Y  I  W  A  O  O  J  N  O  Z  M  L  H  O
```

Name: _____ **Date:** _____

Factors

Factors are numbers that are multiplied to produce a specific product.
For example, 2 and 5 are factors of 10, since $2 \times 5 = 10$.
You can use a factor tree to write a **composite number** as the product of its prime factors. Different factor trees are possible for many composite numbers. It depends on which factor pair you start with. Here are two possible factor trees for the number 48.

> A composite number has factors other than 1 and itself.

Therefore, 48 can be expressed as a product of its **prime factors**.
48 is $2 \times 2 \times 2 \times 2 \times 3$.
The factor pairs of 48 are
1 and 48   2 and 24   3 and 16
4 and 12   6 and 8

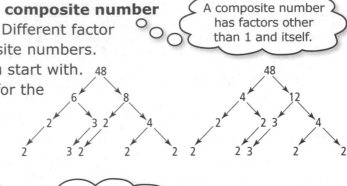

> A prime number has only two different factors, 1 and itself.

1. a) Use a factor tree to write 60 as a product of prime factors.

b) List the factor pairs of 60.

2. List the factor pairs of 12. Show your thinking.

Perimeter and Area

The **perimeter** of a polygon is a measure of the distance around the geometric shape.
The **area** of an object is a measure of how much space a two-dimensional surface covers.
Find the perimeter and area of the rectangle shown.

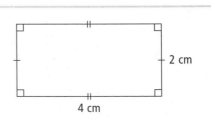

$P = 2l + 2w$ $A = lw$
$P = 2 \times 4 + 2 \times 2$ $A = 4 \times 2$
$P = 8 + 4$ $A = 8$
$P = 12$ The area is 8 cm².
The perimeter is 12 cm.

3. a) Find the perimeter of the polygon.

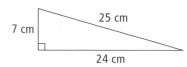

7 cm
25 cm
24 cm

b) What is the area of the polygon?

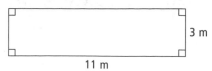

3 m
11 m

Numbers Between

The whole numbers between 9 and 16 are 10, 11, 12, 13, 14, 15.
The difference between 9 and 16 is 7. $16 - 9 = 7$
Half of this difference is 3.5. $7 \div 2 = 3.5$
The number 12.5 is halfway between 9 and 16. $9 + 3.5 = 12.5$

4. List the whole numbers between

   a) 4 and 9   **b)** 25 and 36

5. What number is halfway between each of the numbers in #5?

Solving Equations

An **equation** contains a variable, or unknown value. $x + 5 = 8$
Simple algebraic equations can be solved using $x = 3$
mental math. This method of solving is known
as inspection.

To solve an equation, isolate $5x + 7 = 22$
the variable on one side $5x + 7 - 7 = 22 - 7$ Reverse the addition of 7 by
of the equal sign. When   subtracting 7.
undoing the operations $5x = 15$
performed on the variable, $\dfrac{5x}{5} = \dfrac{15}{5}$ Reverse the multiplication of the
follow the reverse order of   variable with 5 by dividing by 5.
operations. $x = 3$
• subtract and add
• multiply and divide

6. Solve by inspection.

   a) $x + 4 = 11$

7. Solve for x.

   a) $3x = 18$

   b) $2x = 32$

   b) $4x + 1 = 13$

Name: _____ Date: _____

Key Ideas Review

Write the term from column B that matches the correct statement in column A.

A	B
1. A whole number that has only two factors, 1 and itself. _____d_____	**a)** Prime factorization
2. The product of the same two numbers. _____b_____	**b)** Square number
3. The number that equals a given value when you multiply the number by itself. _____e_____	**c)** Perfect square
	d) Prime number
4. The product of the same two factors. _____c_____	**e)** Square root
5. A number written as the product of its prime factors. _____a_____	

Practise and Apply

6. a) Determine the prime factorization of 36. Show your work.

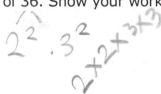

$2^2 \cdot 3^2$
$2 \times 2 \times 3 \times 3$

b) Is 36 a perfect square? Explain your thinking.

Yes $2 \times 3 = 6$
$6 \times 6 = 36$

c) Draw a quadrilateral that shows whether or not 36 is a perfect square. Label its side lengths.

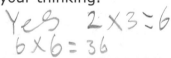

7. Janie's backyard has an area of 100 m².

a) Determine the prime factorization of 100. Show your work.

$2^2 \cdot 5^2$
$2 \times 2 \times 5 \times 5$

b) Is 100 a perfect square? Explain your thinking.

$2\times5=10\times10=100$

$4\times25=100$

c) Draw a quadrilateral that shows whether or not 100 is a perfect square. Label its side lengths.

10

8. Write the prime factorization of each number. Circle the perfect squares.

a) 164

$2\times2\times41$

b) (196)

$2\times2\times7\times7$

c) (225)

$3\times3\times5\times5$

d) 325

$5\times5\times13$

9. Alasie's local football field has an area of 1296 m². Is 1296 a perfect square? Show your thinking.

$24.34=1296$

Perfect square

10. Ingrid says that she knows that 9 and 16 are perfect squares, and that 10 is not. Is she correct? Explain your thinking.

10
2 5

no same two factors

3.2 Exploring the Pythagorean Relationship

MathLinks 8, pages 88–94

Key Ideas Review

Use the diagram below to complete #1.

1. **a)** Write an addition statement to show the relationship
of the squares.

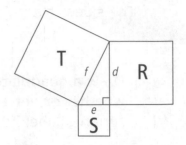

b) Use words to describe the relationship of the squares.

Practise and Apply

2. **a)** What are the areas of the squares
in the diagram? Show your work.

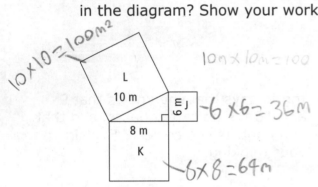

10×10=100m²

10m × 10m = 100

-6 × 6 = 36m

-6 × 8 = 64m

b) Write two addition statements to
show the relationship between
the squares.

3. **a)** Complete the table using
information provided
in the diagram below.

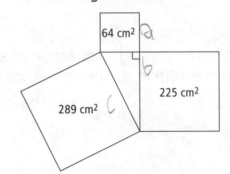

Area of Square	Side Length of Square
64 cm²	8 cm
289 cm²	17 cm
225 cm²	15 cm

b) Show the relationship of the squares.

b)
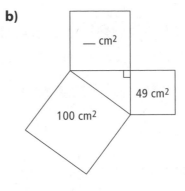

4. The sides of a right triangle measure 15 cm, 20 cm, and 25 cm.

   a) What is the area of each square? Show your work.

   b) Show the relationship of the squares.

5. Is the triangle below a right triangle? Explain your reasoning.

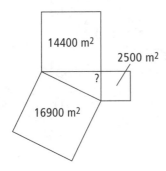

6. Use the Pythagorean relationship to find the unknown area of the squares in the following diagrams. Show your work.

   a)
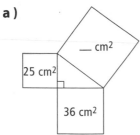

7. What is the area of the square on side *t* of each triangle? Show your work.

   a)   **b)**
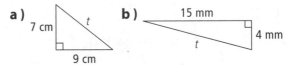

8. Jeremy wants to make sure that the walls he is building are at right angles to each other. He measures and marks 3 m along Wall A, and 4 m along Wall B. The distance between the two marks is 5 m.

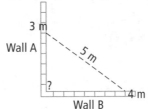

   Are the walls at right angles to each other? Explain how you know.

3.3 Estimating Square Roots

MathLinks 8, pages 95–100

Key Ideas Review

Use your estimating skills to complete #1.

1. **a)** Estimate the square root of 40 using the number line below.

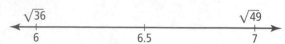

   $\sqrt{36}$ ———————— $\sqrt{49}$
   6   6.5   7

   b) Estimate the whole number that has a square root two thirds of the way along the number line between 3 and 4.

   $\sqrt{9}$ ———— $\sqrt{}$ $\sqrt{16}$
   3   4

2. Complete the following.

   a) When I use a calculator to calculate the square root of a natural number that is a perfect square, I get a _____ number as my answer.

   This is a(n) _____ answer.

   b) When I use a calculator to get the square root of a natural number that is *not* a perfect square, the answer the calculator gives me has

   a _____ in it. This is not an exact answer. It is a(n)

   _____ .

Practise and Apply

3. List the perfect squares immediately before and after the whole number.

	Perfect Square Before	Whole Number	Perfect Square After
a)		5	
b)		18	
c)		78	
d)		95	

4. Identify all of the whole numbers with a square root larger than 5 and smaller than 6.

5. Estimate the square root to one decimal place. Show your work. Check your answer with a calculator.

   a) $\sqrt{17}$

   b) $\sqrt{85}$

Name: _____   **Date:** _____

6. Write the perfect square immediately before and after the whole number, and then estimate the square root of the whole number to one decimal place. Check your estimates with a calculator.

	Perfect Square Before	Whole Number	Perfect Square After	Approx-imate Square Root
a)		27		
b)		55		
c)		105		
d)		140		

7. Martina's painting is on a square canvas with an area of 45 cm². She needs to buy a frame for the painting. Estimate the square's side length to one decimal place. Show your work.

8. Braden's new game board has 225 small squares. All of the small squares form one large square. How many small squares are along one side? Show your work.

9. Chelsea's square garden has an area of 60 m².

a) Estimate to one decimal place the side length of the garden.

b) She has 32 m of fencing to go around the garden. Does she have enough fencing? Explain your thinking.

10. Aaron's parents want to buy an area rug for their 4 m × 4 m living room. They want space around the rug. The rug itself cannot take up more than 90% of the living room. What is the maximum size of rug they can buy? Show your work.

3.4 Using the Pythagorean Relationship

MathLinks 8, pages 101–105

Key Ideas Review

Choose from the following terms to complete #1.

| hypotenuse | legs | length | Pythagorean |

1. The _____ relationship can be used to determine the

_____ of the _____ of a right triangle when

the lengths of the two _____ are known.

2. Use the relationship to determine the length of *C* in each triangle, to the nearest whole number. Show your work.

a)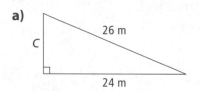

26 m

C

24 m

b)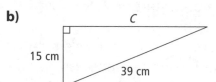

C

15 cm

39 cm

Practise and Apply

3. Determine the length of each hypotenuse. Show your work.

a)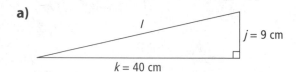

l

j = 9 cm

k = 40 cm

b)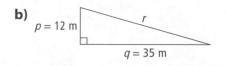

p = 12 m

r

q = 35 m

4. What is the length of each hypotenuse, to the nearest centimetre? Show your work.

a)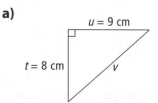

u = 9 cm

t = 8 cm

v

b)

z

x = 6 cm

y = 10 cm

5. Calculate the missing side length for each right triangle, to the nearest tenth of a centimetre. Show your work.

a)

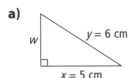

b)

$h = 12$ cm $\quad f = 7$ cm

g

6. Find the height of a triangle with a base of 4 cm and a hypotenuse of 11 cm. Round to the nearest tenth of a centimetre. Show your work.

7. A triangle is made up of two smaller congruent right triangles.

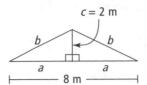

a) Find the length of the hypotenuse for the right triangles, to the nearest tenth of a metre. Show your work.

b) Calculate the perimeter of the large triangle, to the nearest tenth of a metre. Show your work.

8. Ellie and Lucas are going to the skateboard park to try out the new ramp.

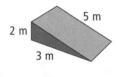

Is the new ramp a right triangle? Explain your thinking.

3.5 Applying the Pythagorean Relationship

MathLinks 8, pages 106–111

Key Ideas Review

Use the diagrams provided to complete the equations for #1.

1. a)

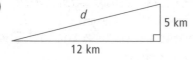

$d^2 = 12^2 +$ _____

$d^2 =$ _____ $+$ _____

$d^2 =$ _____

$d = \sqrt{\rule{2cm}{0pt}}$

$d =$ _____

The hypotenuse is _____ km long.

b)

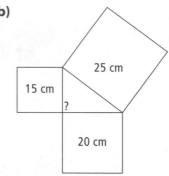

_____ $+$ _____ $=$ _____

Left side: _____ $+$ _____

$=$ _____ $+$ _____

$=$ _____

Right side: _____ $=$ _____

Are both sides equal?
     YES _____   NO _____

Is this a right triangle?
     YES _____   NO _____

Practise and Apply

2. What is the length of the diagonal of a square whose sides measure 9 cm? Give the answer to the nearest tenth of a centimetre. Show your work.

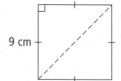

3. Aden decides to swim across a river that is 80 m wide. As he begins to swim the current carries him 60 m downstream. How far did he actually swim?

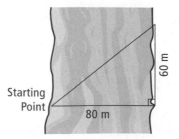

4. The foot of a ladder is 1 m from a wall. If the ladder is 6 m long, how far up the wall does the ladder reach? Give the answer to the nearest tenth of a metre. Show your work.

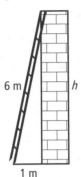

6 m   *h*

1 m

5. The perimeter of an equilateral triangle is 24 cm.

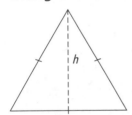

h

Calculate the height of the triangle to the nearest tenth of a centimetre. Show your work.

6. The width of a rectangle is 8 cm, and its diagonal is 17 cm.

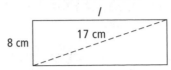

l

8 cm   17 cm

a) Calculate the length of the rectangle. Show your work.

b) Calculate the area of the rectangle. Show your work.

7. A quadrilateral has a width of 17 cm and a length of 26 cm. A diagonal is 31 cm. Is the quadrilateral a rectangle? Justify your answer.

8. A ship leaves port heading due west. After travelling at a speed of 20 km/h for 10 h, the ship makes a 90° turn and heads south, travelling at the same speed. After travelling south for $7\frac{1}{2}$ h, how far is the ship from the port? Show your work.

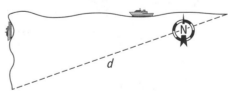

d

Link It Together

1. Complete the table

Perfect Square	Factors	Square Root
a) 16	1, 2, _____, 8, 16	$\sqrt{16} =$ _____
b) 81	1, 3, _____, _____, 81	$\sqrt{81} =$ _____
c) 144	1, _____, _____, 4, _____, _____, _____, 18, 24, _____, _____, 72, 144	$\sqrt{144} =$ _____
d) 225	1, _____, 15, 45, _____	$\sqrt{225} =$ _____
e) 625	_____, 5, _____, _____, 625	$\sqrt{625} =$ _____

2. Two search and rescue boats responded to an SOS off the coast of Tofino. Boat A, which was travelling north at 15 km/h, reached the stranded vessel in 36 minutes. Boat B started from a location directly east of Boat A. It travelled northwest at a speed of 20 km/h and took 45 minutes to reach the stranded vessel.

   a) Draw a diagram that represents the stranded vessel and the search and rescue boats.

   b) Calculate the distance that each search and rescue boat travelled. Show your work.

   c) How far apart were the starting points of Boat A and Boat B? Show your work.

Vocabulary Link

Use the clues to identify the key words from Chapter 3. Then, write them in the crossword puzzle blank.

Across

2. The number 289 is a _____ _____ because $17 \times 17 = 289$.

4. Here is one way of showing the _____ _____: $p^2 = q^2 + r^2$

Down

1. The number 13 is the _____ _____ of 169.

2. This example shows _____ _____: $125 = 5 \times 5 \times 5$

3. Side p is referred to as the _____
of this right triangle.

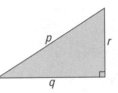

5. Sides q and r are referred to as the _____
of this right triangle.

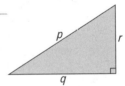

Percents

> *Percent* means out of 100.
> A percent can be represented by shading on a hundred grid.
> This grid represents 53%.

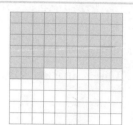

1. What percent is shown on each grid?

a)

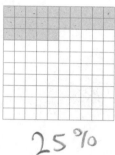

25%

b)

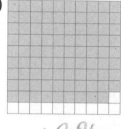

89%

c)

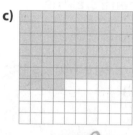

64%

2. Shade hundred grids to represent each percent.

a) 3%

b) 46%

c) 97%

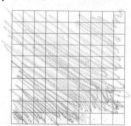

Fractions, Decimals, and Percents

> This diagram represents $\frac{3}{4}$.
> This fraction is 0.75 or 75% of the square.

To change a decimal to a percent, multiply by 100 and add a percent symbol.

3. Show each diagram as a fraction, a decimal, and a percent.

a) 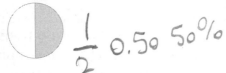 $\frac{1}{4}$ 25% 0.25

b) $\frac{3}{8}$ 0.375 37.5%

c) $\frac{1}{2}$ 0.50 50%

d) $\frac{4}{5}$ 0.8 80%

Repeating Decimals

A *repeating decimal* contains one or more digits that repeat over and over without ending.

$\frac{2}{3} = 0.\overline{6}$ or $2 \div 3 = 0.6666666...$

Use a bar to show the repeating part.

To show as a percent, multiply the decimal by 100 and add a percent symbol.

$0.\overline{6} = 66.\overline{6}\%$

4. Show as repeating decimals.

a) 0.3333333 $0.\overline{333}$

b) 0.4545454 $0.\overline{45}$

c) 0.2727272 $0.\overline{27}$

5. Show each fraction as a repeating decimal and as a percent.

a) $\frac{9}{11}$ $0.\overline{81}$

b) $\frac{7}{9}$ $0.\overline{7}$

c) $\frac{5}{6}$ $0.8\overline{3}$

Estimating Percents

To estimate the percent of a number, use percents you know.

52% of 250 is about 50% of 250.

50% of 250 is half of 250 or 125.

12% of 60 is about 10% of 60.

10% is about one tenth of 60 or 6.

6. Estimate each percent of a number.

a) 22% of 85

25

b) 48% of 102

50

c) 75% of 70

75

d) 82% of 91

75

4.1 Representing Percents
MathLinks 8, pages 122–129

Key Ideas Review

Match each sentence beginning in column A to an ending in column B.

A	B
1. To represent a percent greater than 100%, _C_	a) shade squares from a hundred grid to show the whole number and part of one square to show the fraction.
2. To represent a fractional percent greater than 1%, _a_	
3. To represent a whole percent, _d_	b) shade part of one square on a hundred grid.
4. To represent a fractional percent between 0% and 1%, _b_	c) shade more than one hundred grid.
	d) shade squares on a grid of 100 squares called a hundred grid.

Practise and Apply

5. One full grid represents 100%. What percent does each diagram represent?

a) 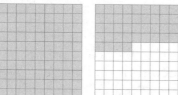 144 %

b) 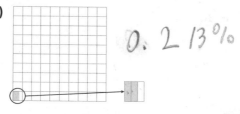 0.213 %

c) 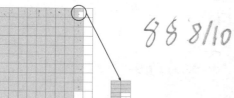 888/10

6. What percent is represented by each diagram if a completely shaded grid represents 100%?

a) 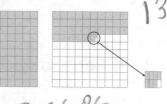 135 1/8

256 %

b)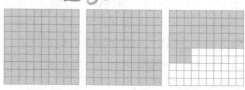

c) 7/12

7. Represent each percent on the grids provided.

a) $\frac{3}{4}$%

b) 174%

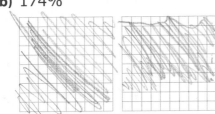

8. Represent the percent in each statement on a grid provided.

a) A tax is $6\frac{1}{2}$%

b) Mt. Everest is about 146% the height of Mt. Logan.

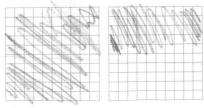

9. How many hundred grids are needed to show each of the following percents? Explain your thinking.

a) 230%

b) 680%

c) 395%

d) 1420%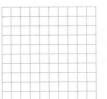

10. About 1.7% of Earth's water is stored in groundwater, lakes, rivers, streams, and soil. Use the hundred grid below to show this percent.

11. An orange contains about 80% of the recommended daily value of vitamin C. Use a hundred grid to show how many oranges you would need to eat to get 100% of the daily value of vitamin C.

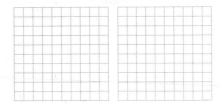

4.2 Fractions, Decimals, and Percents

MathLinks 8, pages 130–137

Key Ideas Review

Choose from the following terms to complete each statement.

decimals   division   fractions   hundred grid   hundred grids   multiplication

1. You can convert fractions to decimals using a ___100 grids___

___grids___ or ___division___.

For example:

$\frac{3}{20}$ = [grid] or ___$=\frac{15}{100}$___

$\frac{3}{20}$ = 3 ÷ 20 = ___0.15___

2. You can convert decimals to percents using ___multipcation___

___division___ or ___fractions___.

For example:

2.26 = [grids] = ___$2\frac{26}{100}$___

2.26 = 2.26 × 100% = ___226___

3. Percents can be written as ___decimals___ and as ___fractions___.

Practise and Apply

4. Rewrite each fraction as a decimal and a percent. Show your thinking.

a) $\frac{3}{4}$ = ___0.75___ or ___75%___

b) $\frac{21}{300}$ = ___0.07___ or ___7___

c) $\frac{9}{5}$ = ___1.8___ or ___180%___

d) $\frac{1}{8}$ = ___0.125___ or ___12.5___

e) $\frac{3}{80}$ = ___0.0375___ or ___3.75___

5. Convert each decimal to a percent and a fraction in lowest terms. Show your thinking.

a) 4.25

4 25

b) 0.845

845

c) 0.0062

0.62

6. Convert each percent to a decimal, then a fraction. Show your thinking.

a) 735%

b) $16\frac{1}{2}\%$

c) 0.6%

7. Tristan charges a flat rate of $16 for each small lawn that he mows. He decided to increase his rate to $20. What is the new rate as a percent of the old rate? Show your thinking.

8. If one completely shaded grid represents one whole, express the shaded portion of each diagram as a fraction, a decimal, and a percent.

a)

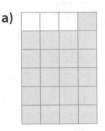

b)

c)

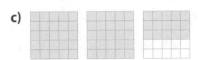

9. About 0.038% of Earth's atmosphere is carbon dioxide. Write this amount as a decimal and a fraction.

10. Kenji calculated that he needed to eat about 2000 calories per day based on his weight, age, and activity level. For lunch, he ate a hamburger that had 538 calories. What percent of Kenji's daily calorie needs does this hamburger represent? Show your thinking.

538 calories

4.3 Percent of a Number

MathLinks 8, pages 138–143

Key Ideas Review

1. Label each example with the mental math strategy it represents: halving, doubling, or dividing by ten. Then, complete the calculation.

   a) 1% of $66

   10% of $66 = $6.60

   So, 1% of 66 = $ [0.66] 0.66 _____

   b) 5% of 180

   10% of 180 = 18

   So, 5% of 180 = [9] _____

   c) 20% of $3.20

   10% of $3.20 = $0.32

   So, 20% of $3.20 = $ [ ] 0.64 _____

2. Circle the terms that correctly complete this statement.
   To calculate the percent of a number, write the percent as a (⟨decimal⟩/fraction), and then (divide/⟨multiply⟩) by the number.

Practise and Apply

3. Use mental math to determine each of the following. Show your thinking.

   a) 200% of 4500
   $100\% = 4500$
   $200\% = 9000$

   b) 0.1% of 600

   c) $1\frac{1}{4}$% of 80

   d) 30% of 70
   21 70

   e) $\frac{4}{5}$% of 15
   12

   f) 450% of 300

4. What is the percent of each number? Give your answer to the nearest hundredth.

a) $\frac{1}{5}$% of 630

b) $23\frac{7}{8}$% of 300

c) 245% of $356.80

d) $68\frac{3}{4}$% of 730

e) 360% of $129.95

5. The commission for the sale of a house was $6\frac{3}{4}$%. If the house sold for $345 000, how much was the commission? Show your thinking.

6. Table salt is a chemical compound of sodium and chlorine. Recommended daily intake is about 1700 mg. If Canadians consume 182% of this amount on average, how much sodium is one person eating daily?

7. Estimate the following answers, then calculate. Show your thinking.

a) Miguel bought a car for $4700. He made a down payment of $19\frac{1}{2}$%. How much was the down payment?

19.5% down

b) About 5.6% of Canadians have Type 2 diabetes. If Canada's population is 32 million, about how many Canadians have this condition?

c) The 4900-seat hockey arena was 63% full. How many people were at the game?

8. The Nile River is about 209% the length of the Yukon River. If the Yukon River is 3168 km, how long is the Nile River (to the nearest km)? Show your work.

Yukon River

Dawson City

Whitehorse

4.4 Combining Percents

MathLinks 8, pages 144–149

5, 6, 8, 9, 10

Key Ideas Review

Match the method of calculating percent in column A with an example in column B.

A	B
1. To determine amounts that result from consecutive percent increases or decreases, percents of percents can be used. _____	a) 111% of 200 = 1.11 × 200 = 222
2. To calculate the increase in a number, multiply the original number by a single percent greater than 100. _____	b) 11% of 200 = 0.11 × 200 = 22 200 + 22 = 222
3. Percents can be combined by adding. _____	c) 5% + 6% = 11%
4. To calculate the increase in a number, add the percent change to the original number. _____	d) 20% of 50 = 10 50 − 10 = 40 20% of 40 = 8 40 − 8 = 32

Practise and Apply

5. Estimate and then calculate each bill, including 13% in taxes.

a) shirt $39.20
   jeans $79.80
   Estimate: 134

   Calculation: 134.47

b) 4 binders $2.25 each
   geometry set $1.65
   calculator $10.35
   Estimate: 24.20

   Calculation: 23.73

c) flashlight $9.75
   3-piece pliers $11.95
   super glue $1.63
   detergent $7.67
   Estimate: 36.80
                  35.03
   Calculation:

d) 2 toothpaste $2.79 each
   3 toothbrushes $7.99 each
   dental floss $4.49
   Estimate: 38.40

   Calculation: 38.47

6. The Casa Della restaurant had 40 diners for lunch on Wednesday. Calculate the number of diners the next night if there was a 15% increase.

$0.15 \times 40 = 6$

$40 + 6 = 46.$ # of diners

7. A clothing store had a 30% off sale one week. The next week, the sale offered another 20% off all jackets.

a) If the original price of a jacket was $120, what was the price in the second week? Show your thinking.

$0.3 \times 120 = 36$ $120 - 36 = 84$
$0.2 \times 84 = 16.8$ $84 - 16.8 =$
                         2 week → 67.2

b) Would a 50% off sale result in a lower price? Explain.

$0.5 \times 120 = 60$ $120 - 60 = 60$

Yes

8. The Electronics for Less store has a 25% off sale on all cameras.

a) What is the sale price of a $240 camera?

$0.25 \times 240 = 60$

$240 - 60 = 180$

b) Find the total cost of the discounted camera including 5% GST and 6% PST. Show your thinking.

$1.11 \times 180 = 199.8$

9. The White Chuck Glacier is in the Cascade Range of western North America. In 1958 it covered 3.1 km^2. By 2002 it had lost about 70% of its area. What was the area of the glacier in 2002? Show your thinking.

$0.7 \times 3.1 = 2.17$ $3.1 - 2.17 = 0.93$

10. Patrick has saved $300 for a new stereo. He finds a $950 stereo on sale for 30% off. If GST is 5% and the PST is 6%, how much money will Patrick have to borrow in order to buy this stereo? Show your thinking.

$950

$0.3 \times 950 = 285$ $950 - 285 = 665$

$1.11 \times 665 = 738.15$

$738.15 - 300 = 438.15$

11. In Mr. Patterson's Math classes, 80% of his 110 students have their own calculators. How many of his students do not have their own calculators? Show your thinking.

$0.8 \times 110 = 88$ $110 - 88 = 22$

12. Sofia started a new job that paid $8/h. In the first two years she was guaranteed a pay raise of 10% every six months. What will be her hourly wage after one year? Show your thinking.

Link It Together

There are 240 students at the school. A concert is being planned. The members of the planning committee are considering different numbers of people that might attend.

1. Complete the table to help them with their thinking.

Scenario	Show Percent Using Hundred Grids	Calculate Size of Possible Audience
a) 80% of the students attend. How large will the audience be?		
b) 71.25% of the students attend. How large will the audience be?		
c) 65% of the students attend. Each student brings a guest. How large will the audience be?		

2. The concert was attended by 75% of the students. $66\frac{2}{3}$% of these students brought two adults.

a) What percent of the school population was accompanied by two adults? Use a hundred grid to show your thinking.

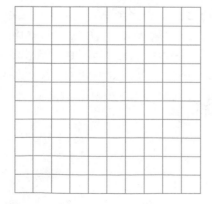

b) How many people attended the concert?

c) Explain why your answer to a) was not $66\frac{2}{3}$% of the school population.

_____

_____

Vocabulary Link

Draw a line from the example in column A to the correct term in column B. Then, find each term in the word search.

A	B
1. 250%	**a)** combined percent
2. 100%	**b)** double
3. 78%	**c)** fractional percent
4. $\frac{3}{200}$%	**d)** greater than one
5. 85% × 2 = 170%	**e)** halve
6. 85% ÷ 2 = 42.5%	**f)** one
7. 40% + 45% = 85%	**g)** percent

```
I G J F R A C T I O N A L P E R C E N T
D T D U J I X P D L C F W J G Q T V C C
M J W P J Q O R Z E W C B O R O H I N T
J S E I I K T L U S V O Y T E O W U A O
D T G O Y E J J E S E M E B A B X D Y O
G S H Y N V C N V T R B L M T O W Z Q M
D Z L M H E B C E H Y I B Z E U J N W W
N M G N D H E L O A S N P E R C E N T G
Y Y S M O T B F J N M E W O T I F S H C
B W H O X U B F Z O A D X Q H E O Z K B
T X I V O S P I W N L P C M A Z P U Q G
S A X D L A J Z Z E L E T D N D E Z F H
I V E U K B D J B B A R Q E O L M P O A
S M E S I R Z E L B M C Y Y N U K H U L
J V K I J F E N Q P O E E L E J Y S A V
W J M H J R F Z X M U N R K O V M C F E
T R W U S Z X R K C N T O O Y E A F G E
R O H J Q R L E J H T S V H N R X Y I U
```

Three-Dimensional Objects

You can describe a three-dimensional (3-D) object by its **faces**, **edges**, and **vertices**.

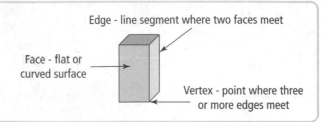

Edge - line segment where two faces meet

Face - flat or curved surface

Vertex - point where three or more edges meet

1. Identify the name and the number of edges, faces, and vertices for each object.

Object	Name	Faces	Edges	Vertices
a)				
b)				
c)				

Circles

A **circle** is a set of points equal distance away from a fixed point, called the centre.

The **radius** is the distance from the centre of a circle to the outside edge. The letter r is often used to represent the radius.

The **diameter** is the distance across a circle through its centre. The letter d is often used to represent the diameter.

The diameter is two times the radius: $d = 2r$. The radius is half the diameter: $r = d\pi^2$.

The distance around a circle is called the **circumference**. The letter C is often used to represent the circumference.

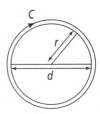

To find the circumference of a circle, use the formula $C = \pi \times d$ or
$C = 2 \times \pi \times r$. Use 3.14 as an approximate value for π.

$C = \pi \times d$ $C = 2 \times \pi \times r$
$C \approx 2 \times 3.14 \times 5$ $C \approx 3.14 \times 10$ The circumference is 3.14
$C \approx 3.14$ $C \approx 3.14$

$C = \pi \times d$
$C \approx 3 \times 10$ M E
$C \approx 30$

The area, A, of a circle is the space the circle encloses.
To find the area of a circle, use the formula $A = \pi \times r^2$ or $A = \pi r^2$.

$A = \pi \times r^2$
$A \approx 3.14 \times 5 \times 5$
$A \approx 78.5$ The area is 78.5 cm².

 r^2 means $r \times r$.

2. a) Find the circumference of the
circle to the nearest tenth of a
centimetre.

7 cm

b) Find the area of the circle to the
nearest tenth of a centimetre
squared.

2 cm

Area Formulas

The **area** is the number of square units needed to cover a surface.

3. Use the formulas to calculate the
area of these shapes to the nearest
tenth of a centimetre squared.

a) Rectangle: $A = l \times w$

$w = 3$ cm
$l = 5.5$ cm

c) Triangle: $A = b \times h \div 2$

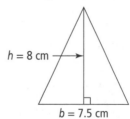
$h = 8$ cm
$b = 7.5$ cm

b) Parallelogram: $A = b \times h$

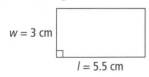
$h = 2.5$ cm
$b = 20$ cm

5.1 Views of Three-Dimensional Objects

MathLinks 8, pages 164–169

Key Ideas Review

Choose from the following terms to complete #1

| build | draw | front | three | 3-D | top | side |

1. **a)** A minimum of _____ views are needed to describe

   _____ objects.

   b) Using the _____, _____, and

   _____ views, you can _____ or

   _____ a _____ object.

2. Lable the views of the item.

_____   _____   _____

Practise and Apply

3. Label each view. Sketch the top, side, and front views.

4. Circle the top view of each object.

a)

b)

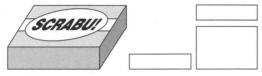

5. Draw and label the top, front, and side views when this table is rotated 90° clockwise.

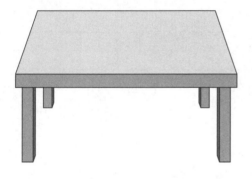

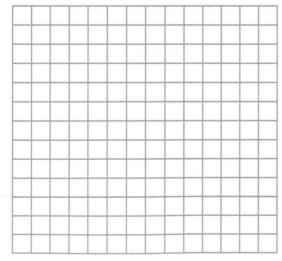

6. Sketch each 3-D object from the three views given.

a)

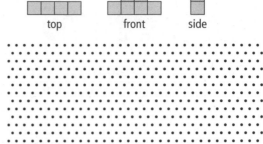

top   front   side

b)

top   front   side

7. Choose the correct top, front, and side view for this object and label each one.

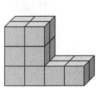

A   B   C

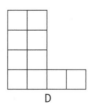

D   E   F

5.2 Nets of Three-Dimensional Objects

MathLinks 8, pages 170–175

Key Ideas Review

1. Complete each statement.

   a) A _____ is a 2-D figure that creates a 3-D object when it is folded.

   b) Different nets can be folded into the same _____

   _____.

Practise and Apply

2. Draw a net for each object.

   a)

   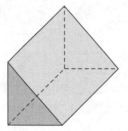

   b)

   c)

   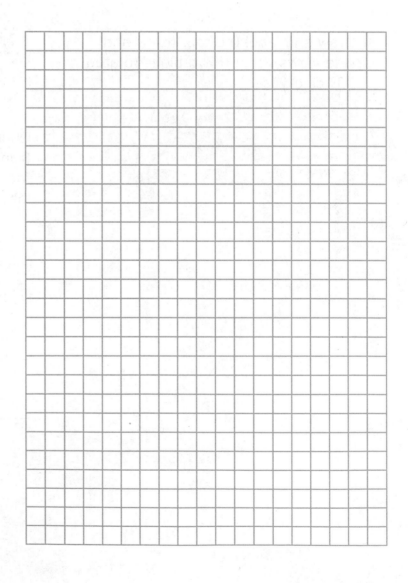

3. Using the grid box, draw a net for a rectangular prism with a length of 8 units, width of 2 units and height of 3 units.

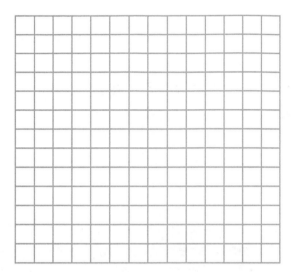

4. Draw at least four possible nets for a cube. (Each net must fold to create a cube.)

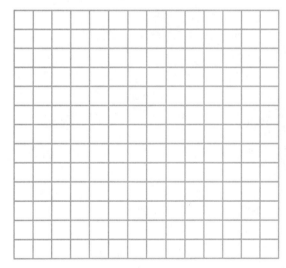

5. Jocelyn is creating a piece of art for her room, using this object as her base. Draw a net of her object so she can do a draft of her design.

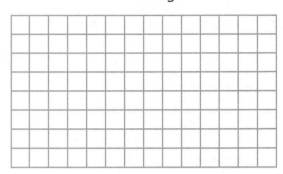

6. A company that manufactures pencils decides to shorten the length of their pencils by 5 cm. A regular pencil measures 19 cm in length.

a) Draw a net of the new pencil with all measurements labelled.

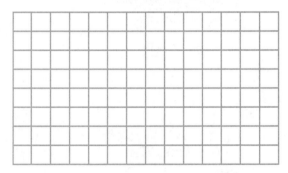

b) Draw a net for a new box that holds ten pencils of the new length. Label your net with all measurements.

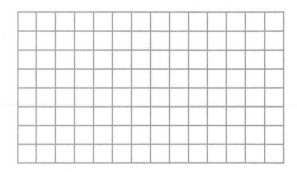

5.3 Surface Area of a Prism

MathLinks 8, pages 176–181

Key Ideas Review

1. Complete the statement.

Finding the sum of all the areas of each _____ on a 3-D object

is called calculating the _____ _____.

Practise and Apply

2. Calculate the surface area of each rectangular prism to the nearest tenth of a centimetre squared.

a)

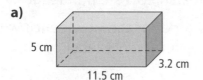

5 cm

3.2 cm

11.5 cm

3. Find the surface area of each triangular prism to the nearest tenth of a meter squared.

a)

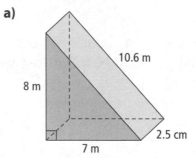

10.6 m

8 m

7 m

2.5 cm

b)

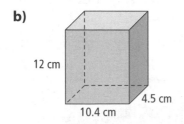

12 cm

4.5 cm

10.4 cm

b)

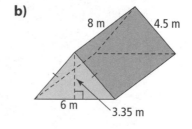

8 m   4.5 m

6 m

3.35 m

4. Ty is painting this storage bench for the deck. How much area does he need to paint, to the nearest hundredth of a square metre?

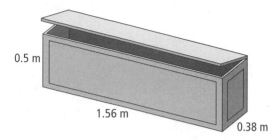

6. The Rileys need to make a new cover for their tent before going camping this summer. Their tent measures 2.2 m in length by 1.6 m wide, and it has a height of 1.1 m.

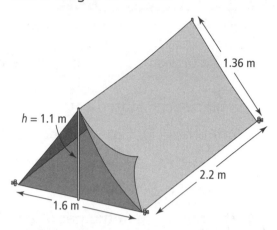

a) Calculate the amount of material they need to make the new cover.

5. Peter needs to paint three boxes for a project. The boxes measure 1.5 m × 1.5 m × 1.5 m, 2.5 m × 2.5 m × 2.5 m, and 3.5 m × 3.5 m × 3.5 m respectively. What is the total surface area that Peter will paint, if he paints the outside of all of the boxes?

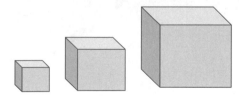

b) Waterproof material at the Fabric Warehouse is on sale this week for $24.95 a square metre. Calculate the cost to make the new cover.

5.4 Surface Area of a Cylinder

MathLinks 8, pages 182–187

Key Ideas Review

Choose from the following terms to complete #1.

| 3-D object | add | area | circumference | cylinder |

1. Complete each statement.

   a) To find the surface area of a cylinder, you _____ the

      _____ of each face of the object.

   b) A net of a _____ is made up of three faces.

   c) The rectangle in the net of a cylinder uses the _____ of the

      circle as one dimension.

Practise and Apply

2. Sketch a net for this cylinder.

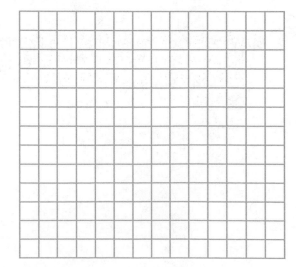

3. Estimate the surface area for each cylinder.

   a)

   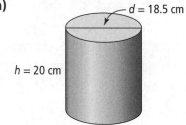

   $d = 18.5$ cm

   $h = 20$ cm

   b)

   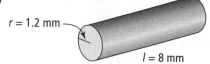

   $r = 1.2$ mm

   $l = 8$ mm

4. Calculate the surface area of this cylinder to the nearest hundredth of a square centimetre.

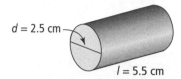

$d = 2.5$ cm

$l = 5.5$ cm

5. Use the following formula to find the surface area of each cylinder to the nearest hundredth of a square unit.

$$SA = (2 \times \pi \times r^2) + (\pi \times d \times h)$$

a)

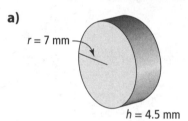

$r = 7$ mm

$h = 4.5$ mm

b)

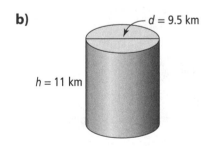

$d = 9.5$ km

$h = 11$ km

6. Recordable disks come in bulk packaging of various sizes.

A single compact disk has a diameter of 12 cm and a width of 0.1 cm.

a) Calculate the surface area of one compact disk to the nearest tenth of a centimetre squared.

b) Calculate the surface area of a bulk container that holds 50 compact disks. Explain your reasoning.

Link It Together

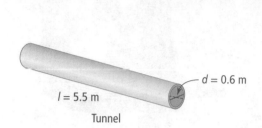

Tunnel

$l = 5.5$ m $d = 0.6$ m

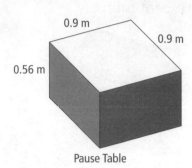

0.9 m

0.9 m

0.56 m

Pause Table

You have been asked to make two parts of the Dog Agility course for this year's competition. One piece is a tunnel made out of durable nylon that the dogs run through. The other piece is a cube to be used as a pause table. The dogs must stay stationary on this table for a fixed amount of time.

1. Sketch the top, front, and side view of each piece.

2. Draw a net of each.

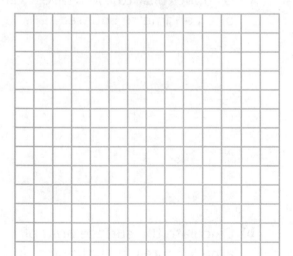

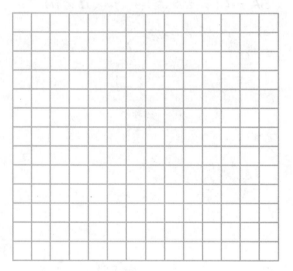

3. Calculate the surface area of each piece to the nearest hundredth of a square metre.

Vocabulary Link

Use the visuals or explanation to identify the key words from Chapter 5. Then, write them in the crossword puzzle blank.

Across

4.

6.

Down

1. Is the number of square units needed to cover a 3-D object.

3.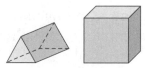

2.

5.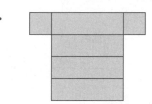

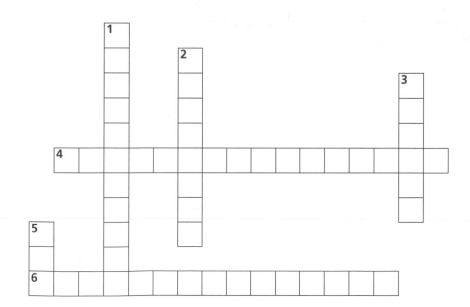

Name: _____ Date: _____

Add and Subtract Fractions

To add fractions with like denominators, add the numerators.

$\frac{1}{5}$

$+ \frac{2}{5}$

$= \frac{3}{5}$

Each fraction in the above sum is a **proper fraction**, because the denominator is greater than the numerator.

To subtract fractions with unlike denominators, use a **common denominator**. This is a common multiple of the denominators.

$\frac{1}{2} - \frac{1}{6} =$

$\frac{3}{6}$

$- \frac{1}{6}$

$= \frac{2}{6}$

Write the answer in lowest terms.

$\div\ ?$

$\frac{2}{6} = \frac{1}{3}$

$\div\ ?$

What is a common factor of 2 and 6?

1. Add. Write each answer in lowest terms.

   a) $\frac{1}{6} + \frac{1}{6} = \frac{2}{6} = \frac{1}{3}$

   b) $\frac{1}{2} + \frac{1}{3}$ $\frac{3}{6} + \frac{2}{6} = \frac{5}{6}$

   c) $\frac{3}{10} + \frac{2}{5}$ $\frac{3}{10} + \frac{4}{10} = \frac{7}{10}$

2. Subtract. Write each answer in lowest terms.

   a) $\frac{7}{8} - \frac{5}{8}$ $\frac{2}{8} = \frac{1}{4}$

   b) $\frac{4}{5} - \frac{3}{10}$ $\frac{8}{10} - \frac{3}{10} = \frac{5}{10} = \frac{1}{2}$

   c) $\frac{4}{5} - \frac{2}{3}$ $\frac{12}{15} - \frac{10}{15} = \frac{2}{15}$

Add and Subtract Mixed Numbers

A **mixed number** includes a whole number and a fraction.
Write the improper fraction as a mixed number.

$$1\frac{3}{8} + 2\frac{7}{8} = 3 + \frac{10}{8} = 3 + \frac{8}{8} + \frac{2}{8}$$

To subtract mixed numbers, use a common denominator.

$$4\frac{1}{2} - 2\frac{3}{4} = 4\frac{2}{4} - 2\frac{3}{4}$$

If the second fraction is bigger than the first, use one of the following methods.

Literacy Link

An improper fraction has a numerator greater than the denominator.

Use an Improper Fraction

$$4\frac{2}{4} - 2\frac{3}{4} = \frac{18}{4} - \frac{11}{4}$$
$$= \frac{7}{4}$$
$$= 1\frac{3}{4}$$

Use Regrouping

Regroup 1 whole from $4\frac{2}{4}$.

$$4\frac{2}{4} = 3 + \frac{4}{4} + \frac{2}{4}$$
$$= 3 + \frac{6}{4}$$
$$3\frac{6}{4} - 2\frac{3}{4} = 1\frac{3}{4}$$

Subtract the whole numbers and subtract the fractions.

3. Add or subtract. Write each answer in lowest terms.

   a) $1\frac{1}{5} + 2\frac{3}{5} = 3\frac{4}{5}$

   b) $3\frac{1}{4} + 2\frac{3}{4} = 5\frac{4}{4} = 6$

   c) $2\frac{3}{5} - 1\frac{2}{5} = 1\frac{1}{5}$

   d) $2\frac{6}{7} + 2\frac{4}{7} = 4\frac{10}{7} = \frac{39}{7} = 7$

4. Add. Write each answer in lowest terms.

   a) $1\frac{5}{8} + 2\frac{3}{4}$ $\frac{13}{8} + \frac{11}{4} = \frac{13}{8} + \frac{22}{8} = \frac{35}{8} = 4\frac{3}{8}$

   b) $3\frac{1}{2} + 3\frac{4}{5}$ $\frac{7}{2} + \frac{19}{5} = \frac{35}{10} + \frac{38}{10} = \frac{73}{10} = 7\frac{3}{10}$

5. Subtract. Write each answer in lowest terms.

   a) $3\frac{1}{2} - 1\frac{1}{3}$ $\frac{3}{6} - \frac{2}{6} = 2\frac{1}{6}$

   b) $3\frac{3}{4} - 1\frac{1}{2}$ $\frac{3}{4} - \frac{2}{4} = 2\frac{1}{4}$

Order of Operations

The **order of operations** is the correct sequence of steps for a calculation.

$30 - 14 \div (5 - 3) \times 4 + 6$ Do brackets first.
$= 30 - 14 \div 2 \times 4 + 6$ Multiply and divide, from left to right.
$= 30 - 28 + 6$ Add and subtract, from left to right.
$= 8$

6. Calculate. Show your thinking.

   a) $3 - 12 \div 2 + 4$ b) $8 + 18 \div 3 - 2 \times (4 + 1)$

6.1 Multiplying a Fraction and a Whole Number

MathLinks 8, pages 198–203

Key Ideas Review

For #1 and #2, unscramble the letters to form a word that correctly completes the statement. Then, complete the examples.

1. Manipulatives and diagrams can be used to model a ___multipcatioq___
   ACIIILLMNOPTTU
   statement.

   a) $4 \times \dfrac{\boxed{1}}{\boxed{3}} = 1\dfrac{\boxed{1}}{\boxed{3}}$

   b) $3 \times \dfrac{\boxed{1}}{\boxed{2}} = 1\dfrac{\boxed{1}}{\boxed{2}}$

   c) $4 \times \dfrac{\boxed{3}}{4} = \dfrac{\boxed{12}}{4} = \boxed{3}$

2. Multiplying a ___fraction___ and a whole number in
   ACFINORT

   ___either___ order gives the same result.
   EEHIRT

   $6 \times \dfrac{2}{3} = 4$ $\dfrac{\boxed{2}}{\boxed{3}} \times 6 = 4$

Practise and Apply

3. Write the multiplication statement that each diagram represents. A ⬡ represents one whole.

   a) △ △ △ △ = ◇ ◇

      = ◇ ◇

      $4 \times$

   b) △ △ △ = ⬡ ◇

   c) ▢ ▢ ▢ ▢ = ⬡ ◇

4. Write the multiplication statement represented by each diagram.

a)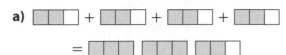

b)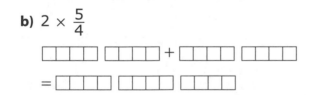

c)

5. Shade each set of diagrams to determine the product.

a) $3 \times \frac{2}{5}$

b) $2 \times \frac{5}{4}$

6. Complete each number line to determine the product.

a) $6 \times \frac{1}{3}$

b) $8 \times \frac{1}{9}$

7. Determine each product. Show your thinking.

a) $3 \times \frac{1}{4}$

b) $5 \times \frac{1}{8}$

c) $4 \times \frac{1}{2}$

d) $3 \times \frac{5}{3}$

e) $2 \times \frac{3}{4}$

8. In the her first week on the job, Trindis worked 9 hours. In the second week she worked $\frac{2}{3}$ of that amount. Complete the number line to determine how many hours Trindis worked in the second week.

9. Marik had 11 friends at his birthday party. Each person ate $\frac{1}{4}$ of a pizza. How many pizza's did Marik and his friends eat? Write a multiplication statement to answer the question, then find the product.

10. Jeremy ran around a 150-m track $1\frac{1}{2}$ times. Show two different methods of finding the product of $1\frac{1}{2} \times 150$. How far did Jeremy run?

6.2 Dividing a Fraction by a Whole Number

MathLinks 8, pages 204–209

Key Ideas Review

Match each model in column B to a division statement in column A.

A	B
1. $\frac{1}{3} \div 3$ _____	**a)** ![number line from 0 to 1 with marks at 1/5, 2/5, 3/5, 4/5] 0 $\frac{1}{5}$ $\frac{2}{5}$ $\frac{3}{5}$ $\frac{4}{5}$ 1
2. $\frac{5}{6} \div 4$ _____	**b)**
3. $\frac{4}{5} \div 2$ _____	**c)**

Practise and Apply

4. Determine each quotient. Use the pattern blocks to show your thinking. In this question, ⬡ represents 1 whole.

a) $\frac{1}{2} \div 3$

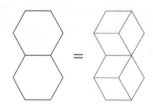

b) $\frac{5}{6} \div 2$

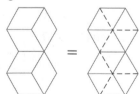

5. Determine each quotient. Use the fraction strips to show your thinking.

a) $\frac{1}{3} \div 4$

b) $\frac{5}{6} \div 3$

6. Determine each quotient by completing the number lines.

   a) $\frac{2}{3} \div 3$

   b) $\frac{3}{5} \div 2$

7. Jim and two friends offered to help Jim's father paint a room. There is $\frac{2}{3}$ of a can of paint left. If the paint is shared evenly, how much paint will each person get?

   a) Write a division statement to answer this problem.

   b) Use a model to determine the quotient.

8. A board that is $\frac{3}{5}$ of a metre long is cut in half. What fraction of a metre is each piece?

   a) Write a division statement to answer this problem.

   b) Use a model to determine the quotient.

9. Teresa finds $\frac{9}{12}$ of a chocolate bar to share with 3 friends. What fraction of a chocolate bar does each person get?

   a) Write a division statement to answer this problem.

   b) Use a model to determine the quotient.

6.3 Multiplying Proper Fractions

MathLinks 8, **pages 210–215**

Key Ideas Review

Choose from the following terms to complete #1 to #3.

estimate	multiply	numerators	paper folding

1. Two proper fractions can be multiplied using _____ or diagrams.

2. A rule for multiplying two proper fractions is to multiply the

   _____ and _____ the denominators.

3. You can _____ the product of two proper fractions by first

   deciding whether each fraction is closer to 0, $\frac{1}{2}$, or 1.

Practise and Apply

4. Estimate and calculate each product. Show your thinking and express your answer in lowest terms.

   a) $\frac{2}{3} \times \frac{5}{6}$

   Circle the closest estimate: 0 $\frac{1}{2}$ 1

   b) $\frac{4}{9} \times \frac{1}{5}$

   Circle the closest estimate: 0 $\frac{1}{2}$ 1

   c) $\frac{2}{5} \times \frac{3}{8}$

   Circle the closest estimate: 0 $\frac{1}{2}$ 1

   d) $\frac{2}{3} \times \frac{3}{5}$

   Circle the closest estimate: 0 $\frac{1}{2}$ 1

   e) $\frac{7}{8} \times \frac{3}{5}$

   Circle the closest estimate: 0 $\frac{1}{2}$ 1

   f) $\frac{9}{10} \times \frac{8}{9}$

   Circle the closest estimate: 0 $\frac{1}{2}$ 1

5. Tamara lives $\frac{3}{4}$ km from school. She runs $\frac{1}{3}$ of the distance and then walks the rest of the way to her house. How far does Tamara run? Show your thinking.

6. In a grade 8 class, $\frac{1}{2}$ of the students play piano. Of these students, $\frac{1}{4}$ also play guitar. What fraction of this class play both piano and guitar?

7. On a Saturday, Sid helped his father do yard work for $\frac{5}{6}$ of the afternoon. He mowed lawn for $\frac{3}{5}$ of this time. What fraction of the afternoon did Sid spend mowing the lawn? Estimate, then solve.

   Estimate:

   Solution:

8. Vancouver's population is approximately $\frac{2}{5}$ the population of Toronto. Québec City's population is approximately $\frac{1}{3}$ of Vancouver's population. Compare Québec City's population to Toronto's population.

9. Hayden's hard drive is $\frac{2}{5}$ filled. The operating system takes up $\frac{1}{10}$ of that space. How much of the whole hard drive is filled by the operating system? Use a model to show your thinking.

10. An order of bruschetta for 4 uses $\frac{1}{3}$ of a loaf of French bread. How much of a loaf does each person get when they share the order equally?

6.4 Multiplying Improper Fractions and Mixed Numbers

MathLinks 8, pages 216–221

Key Ideas Review

1. Decide whether each of the following statements is true or false. Circle the word *True* or *False*. If the statement is false, rewrite it to make It true.

   a) **True/False** You can model the multiplication of two mixed numbers or improper fractions using partial areas of a rectangle.

   _____

   _____

   b) **True/False** You can calculate the product of two mixed numbers or improper fractions by multiplying the whole numbers closest to them.

   _____

   _____

   c) **True/False** Two mixed numbers can be multiplied by expressing them as improper fractions and then multiplying the numerators by the denominators.

   _____

   _____

Practise and Apply

2. Express each improper fraction as a mixed number.

   a) $\frac{9}{5}$ b) $\frac{13}{6}$

3. Express each mixed number as an improper fraction.

   a) $2\frac{1}{2}$ b) $4\frac{2}{3}$

4. Use a model to determine each product.

   a) $1\frac{1}{2} \times \frac{1}{3}$ b) $1\frac{1}{3} \times 2\frac{1}{4}$

5. Estimate and calculate. Show your thinking.

   a) $\frac{2}{3} \times \frac{6}{5}$

   Estimate: _____

   Calculate:

   b) $4 \times 2\frac{1}{3}$

   Estimate: _____

   Calculate:

   c) $1\frac{3}{4} \times 3\frac{1}{3}$

   Estimate: _____

   Calculate:

6. One week, Kristi worked 3 days at a department store for $3\frac{1}{2}$ h each day. She was paid $9/h.

   a) How many hours did Kristi work that week? Show your thinking.

   b) How much did Kristi earn that week?

7. Jupiter completes about $2\frac{2}{5}$ rotations every 24 hours (an Earth day). How many rotations does Jupiter complete in one Earth week? Show your thinking.

8. A sailboat is sailing at $8\frac{1}{2}$ km/h. If the weather conditions and the current do not change, how far will the sailboat travel in $1\frac{1}{3}$ h? Show your thinking.

9. The distance to Grandma's house is $\frac{4}{5}$ of the distance to Uncle Glen's house. If Uncle Glen's house is $3\frac{1}{2}$ hours away, how long will it take to get to Grandma's house if you travel at the same speed?

10. It takes $\frac{3}{5}$ of a tank of gas to get to work and back each day. How much gas is used over 5 work days? Show your thinking.

11. Owen is $2\frac{1}{4}$ times as old as Robin. When Robin celebrates his 8th birthday, how old will Owen be?

12. The karate club is arranging a grading for its members. It takes $3\frac{1}{4}$ hours to test a group of 4 candidates. How long will the club need the gym in order to process 3 groups of 4 candidates each?

6.5 Dividing Fractions and Mixed Numbers

MathLinks 8, pages 222–229

Key Ideas Review

Match each method in column A with the example in column B that best matches it.

A	B
1. Use diagrams to estimate the quotient of two fractions. _____	**a)** $3\frac{3}{4} \div 1\frac{1}{2} = \frac{15}{4} \div \frac{3}{2}$ $= \frac{15}{4} \div \frac{6}{4}$ $= \frac{15}{6}$ or $2\frac{1}{2}$
2. Estimate the quotient of two improper fractions or mixed numbers by dividing the whole numbers closest to them. _____	**b)**
3. Divide two fractions by writing them with a common denominator, and dividing the numerators. _____	**c)** $5\frac{1}{5} \div 1\frac{2}{3} \approx 5 \div 2$ $\approx \frac{5}{2}$ or $2\frac{1}{2}$
4. Divide a fraction by multiplying by its reciprocal. _____	**d)** $\frac{3}{5} \div \frac{6}{7} = \frac{3}{5} \times \frac{7}{6}$ $= \frac{21}{30} = \frac{7}{10}$

Practise and Apply

5. Complete the diagrams to determine each quotient.

a) $\frac{5}{6} \div \frac{1}{3}$

b) $1\frac{1}{2} \div \frac{3}{4}$

c) $\frac{1}{3} \div \frac{1}{2}$

d) $1\frac{3}{4} \div \frac{2}{3}$

6. Divide using a common denominator. Show your thinking.

a) $\frac{2}{3} \div \frac{5}{6}$

b) $1\frac{7}{8} \div \frac{3}{4}$

c) $3\frac{3}{10} \div 2\frac{2}{5}$

d) $1\frac{2}{3} \div 2\frac{5}{9}$

7. Divide using multiplication.

a) $\frac{5}{8} \div \frac{2}{3}$

b) $7 \div 4\frac{2}{3}$

c) $1\frac{5}{6} \div \frac{7}{12}$

d) $6\frac{2}{3} \div 2\frac{1}{2}$

8. Estimate, then divide using a common denominator. Show your thinking.

   a) $1\frac{7}{8} \div 1\frac{1}{4}$ Estimate: _____
   Calculate:

   b) $5\frac{7}{10} \div 3\frac{9}{10}$ Estimate: _____
   Calculate:

   c) $2\frac{1}{6} \div 1\frac{5}{12}$ Estimate: _____
   Calculate:

9. Estimate, then divide using multiplication. Show your thinking.

   a) $6\frac{5}{6} \div 3\frac{1}{2}$ Estimate: _____
   Calculate:

   b) $8\frac{1}{3} \div 2\frac{3}{4}$ Estimate: _____
   Calculate:

   c) $7\frac{1}{8} \div 4$ Estimate: _____
   Calculate:

10. Carlos got $\frac{5}{6}$ of the test questions correct. This was 15 questions. How many questions were on the test? Show your thinking.

11. Alisha needed $\frac{3}{4}$ L of gasoline to mow the lawn. There was $3\frac{3}{4}$ L of gasoline in the container. How many times can she mow the lawn before refilling the container? Show your thinking.

12. Jean-Pierre walked $4\frac{1}{2}$ km in $1\frac{1}{4}$ h. If he walked at a steady pace, how fast did he walk in kilometres per hour? Show your thinking.

13. A running track used in competition is $\frac{2}{5}$ km. How many laps is the 1500 m race? Show two ways to solve the problem.

   There are 1000 m in 1 km.

6.6 Applying Fraction Operations

MathLinks 8, pages 230–235

Key Ideas Review

1. Circle the correct response to complete each statement.

   a) You need to decide which (operation/manipulation) to perform on fractions to solve problems.

   b) Some fraction problems can involve the (computation/order) of operations.

2. Number the statements to put the operations in the correct order.

   _____ Add and subtract in order from left to right.

   _____ Brackets

   _____ Multiply and divide in order from left to right.

Practise and Apply

3. Circle the first step in calculating the answer, then solve.

   a) $\frac{5}{6} - \frac{1}{3} \times \frac{3}{4}$

   b) $3\frac{1}{2} \div \frac{3}{4} - \left(1\frac{1}{2} + \frac{5}{6}\right)$

   c) $\frac{7}{8} + \frac{2}{3} - \frac{1}{4}$

   d) $1\frac{1}{2} \times \frac{1}{3} \div \frac{2}{3}$

4. Calculate. Show your thinking.

   a) $3 \div \frac{3}{4} + 5 \times \frac{1}{2}$

   b) $\frac{2}{3} + \frac{1}{6} \times 1\frac{2}{3}$

   c) $\frac{3}{4} \times (12 - 8) - \frac{3}{8}$

   d) $3\frac{7}{10} \div \left(1\frac{3}{10} + 1\frac{9}{10}\right)$

5. Tracy earns $12 an hour as a cashier in a grocery store. One week she worked 8 hours a day for 5 days. One of these days was a holiday, for which she earned time-and-a-half. How much did Tracy earn that week?

6. Graham saved $1\frac{1}{2}$ bags of Halloween candy to share with two friends. Graham's father asked him to save $\frac{1}{4}$ of a bag for his younger brother. If Graham and his friends each get equal amounts of what is left, how much candy will each of them get?

7. Add one pair of brackets to the left side of each equation to make it true.

a) $\frac{1}{2} + \frac{5}{8} \times \frac{4}{3} + \frac{3}{2} = 3$

b) $1\frac{1}{4} - \frac{1}{8} \div 1\frac{1}{2} - \frac{3}{4} = 1\frac{1}{12}$

c) $\frac{13}{5} - \frac{3}{10} + \frac{7}{10} \div \frac{1}{2} - \frac{3}{5} = 0$

d) $1\frac{1}{4} \times 2\frac{2}{5} \div 2\frac{1}{6} - 1\frac{1}{3} = \frac{2}{39}$

8. Here is a way of using four 3s and the order of operations to write an expression that equals 5.

$$3 - \frac{3}{3} + 3 = 5$$

Use four 3s and the order of operations to write expressions with each of the following values.

a) 0

b) 1

c) 2

d) 3

9. Lake Huron has about 2000 km of shoreline. Lake Superior's shoreline is $\frac{1}{2}$ plus $\frac{1}{5}$ of that distance. Write an expression to determine the length of shoreline in Lake Superior, then solve.

Link It Together

The school band sold juice at the dance as a fundraiser. They bought a concentrate that cost $2/L. Each litre of concentrate made 4 L of juice. The sizes of the drinks, the cost of each drink, and the number sold are shown in the table.

Size of Drink	Price	Number Sold
Small $\left(\frac{1}{6} \text{ L}\right)$	$0.50	16
Medium $\left(\frac{1}{4} \text{ L}\right)$	$0.75	27
Large $\left(\frac{1}{2} \text{ L}\right)$	$1.00	13

1. How much juice was sold?

   a) Estimate the answer. Show your thinking.

   b) Calculate.

2. How much money did they raise? Show your thinking.

3. The band bought enough concentrate to make 20 L of juice. How much concentrate did they buy? Use a model to show your thinking.

4. What profit did the band make? Justify your response.

Vocabulary Link

Unscramble the letters of each term. The terms are one to three words long. Use the clues to help you solve the puzzles.

A	B
1. $\frac{3}{4}$ ← _____	ONODTRIEMAN
2. For $\frac{5}{6}$, this would be $\frac{6}{5}$. _____	AOPCELRCIR
3. You can add or multiply two numbers in any order. For example, $a + b = b + a$ and $a \times b = b \times a$. _____	RTUEECIOOMPPVMATYRT
4. $\frac{11}{12}$ ← _____	EANTRMROU
5. $\frac{2}{3}$ _____	ETRNOPRRFAPCIO
6. answer to a division question _____	OETNQITU
7. answer to a multiplication question _____	DURTOPC
8. This would include the following list: • brackets • multiply and divide in order • add and subtract in order _____	DEREROROFOIONPATS
9. $2\frac{4}{5}$ _____	BENIMEXMDUR
10. number you are dividing into _____	DDDNIIEV
11. $\frac{15}{6}$ _____	PERPINCFOMORRIAT
12. number you are dividing by _____	SIIODVR

Name: _____ **Date:** _____

Identifying Right Cylinders and Right Prisms

Right prisms and right cylinders have lateral faces that meet the base at 90°.

This is a right cylinder.   This is not a right cylinder.

face
base

1. Identify the right prisms and right cylinders. Explain how you know.

a)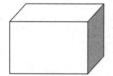

b)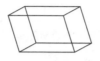

c)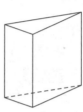

d)

e)

f)

Use Mental Math

Mental mathematics includes estimating answers mentally.

When you are asked to estimate, give an approximate but carefully thought-out answer.

To estimate 58 × 3.7, use numbers that are easy to work with.

50 × 3 = 150 Use front-end estimation.
60 × 4 = 240 Use relative size estimation.
60 × 3 = 180 Round one up and the other down.
The answer to 58 × 3.7 is between 150 and 240.

2. Estimate each answer. Show your thinking.
   a) 7.6 × 24

   b) 96 × 8.1

   c) 2.9 × 68

Calculating Area

Area measures the region inside a two-dimensional space.
This rectangle has a shaded triangle.
What is the area of the remaining part
of the rectangle?

Area of rectangle = $l \times w$

$$A = 40 \times 13$$
$$A = 520$$

The area of the rectangle is 520 cm².

Area of triangle = $(b \times h) \div 2$

$$A = (10 \times 13) \div 2$$
$$A = 130 \div 2$$
$$A = 65$$

The area of the triangle is 65 cm².

Area of unshaded region = Area of rectangle – Area of triangle

$$A = 520 - 65$$
$$A = 455$$

The area of the unshaded region is 455 cm².

40 cm

13 cm

10 cm

3. Calculate the area of each shaded region. Round your answers to the nearest tenth.

a)

26 cm

32 cm

b)

6 m

c)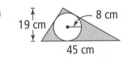

19 cm   8 cm

45 cm

Repeated Multiplication

6² can be written as 6 × 6.

$$6^2 = 6 \times 6$$
$$= 36$$

6^2 is read as "6 squared" or "6 to the power of 2"

2³ can be written as 2 × 2 × 2.

$$2^3 = 2 \times 2 \times 2$$
$$= 8$$

2^3 is read as "2 cubed" or "2 to the power of 3"

4. Write as repeated multiplication, then calculate each answer.

   a) 4^3 b) 3^5

5. Is 3^4 the same as 4^3? Justify your response.

7.1 Understanding Volume

MathLinks 8, pages 246–253

Key Ideas Review

Choose from the following terms to complete #1.

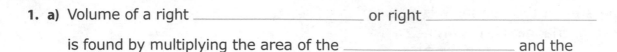

| base | cylinder | does | does not | height | prism |

1. **a)** Volume of a right _____ or right _____

   is found by multiplying the area of the _____ and the

   _____.

   b) If you change the orientation, it _____ affect the volume.

2. **a)** Shade the base of each right cylinder.

    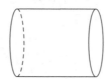

   b) Shade the base of each right triangular prism.

Practise and Apply

3. Use the figure measurements to calculate the volume.

   a)

   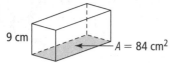

   9 cm

   $A = 84$ cm^2

   $V =$ _____ × _____

   $V =$ _____

   b)

   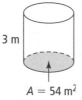

   3 m

   $A = 54$ m^2

   $V =$ _____ × _____

   $V =$ _____

4. Calculate the volume of each prism or cylinder.

a)

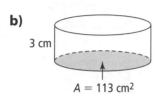

4 cm $A = 100$ cm²

b)

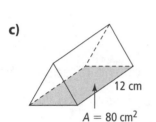

3 cm $A = 113$ cm²

c)

12 cm $A = 80$ cm²

5. What is the volume of a right prism that has a base with an area of 15 cm² and a height of 7 cm?

6. Which rectangular prism has the larger volume? Show your thinking.

a)

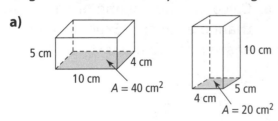

5 cm   4 cm   10 cm
10 cm $A = 40$ cm²
$A = 20$ cm²   5 cm   4 cm

b)

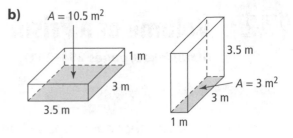

$A = 10.5$ m²   1 m   3.5 m   3.5 m $A = 3$ m²   3 m   3.5 m   1 m

7. Calculate the height of each rectangular prism.

a) volume = 63 cm³
area of base = 9 cm²

b) volume = 26 m³
area of base = 4 m²

8. Nikki and Taylor have to fill the pool this summer. The area of the pool bottom is 27 m². The height that the water needs to be is 0.9 m. How much water do they need to put in the pool?

9. Chad wants to cut back on the amount of treats he is eating. He has two chocolate bars to choose from. Which one has less chocolate? Show your thinking.

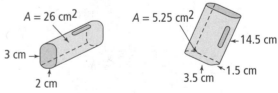

$A = 26$ cm² $A = 5.25$ cm²   14.5 cm
3 cm   1.5 cm
2 cm   3.5 cm

7.2 Volume of a Prism

MathLinks 8, pages 254–261

Key Ideas Review

Draw a line to connect each object from column B with the correct formula in column A.

A	B
1. $V = l \times w \times h$	**a)** Cube
2. $V = (b \times h \div 2) \times h$	**b)** Right rectangular prism
3. $V = s \times s \times s$	**c)** Right triangular prism

Practise and Apply

4. Calculate the volume of each rectangular prism.

a) $l = 15$ cm, $w = 12$ cm, $h = 3$ cm

b)

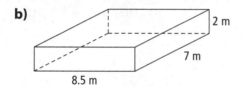

8.5 m, 7 m, 2 m

c)

20 cm, 8 cm, 16 cm

5. Calculate the volume of each cube.

a) Express your answer to the nearest tenth.

4.5 cm

b) $s = 7$ cm

6. Calculate the volume of each right triangular prism. Express your answer to the nearest tenth.

a)

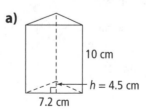

10 cm, $h = 4.5$ cm, 7.2 cm

b)

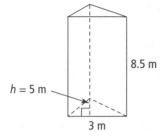

8.5 m

$h = 5$ m

3 m

c) A prism where the base of the triangle is 4 m, the height of the triangle is 5 m, and the prism height is 12 m.

7. Calculate the volume of the contents of each container.

a) $\frac{3}{4}$ full

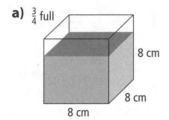

8 cm

8 cm

8 cm

b)

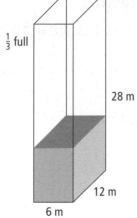

$\frac{1}{3}$ full

28 m

12 m

6 m

c) $\frac{3}{8}$ full

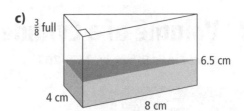

6.5 cm

4 cm

8 cm

8. Wab needs to buy drinks for the summer barbeque. Both containers are the same price. Which one holds more? Show your thinking.

Juice   4.5 cm

6 cm   9 cm

Juice   3.75 cm

10 cm   6 cm

9. A contractor is buying cement for 100 triangular parking barriers. How much concrete does she need?

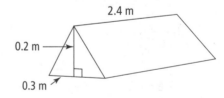

2.4 m

0.2 m

0.3 m

7.3 Volume of a Cylinder
MathLinks 8, pages 262–267

Key Ideas Review

Choose from the following terms to complete #1 to #3.

area	circle	cylinder	volume

1. The shape of the base of a cylinder is a _____.

2. The formula for the _____ of a

   _____ is $A = \pi \times r^2$.

3. The formula for the _____ of a _____ is

   $V =$ _____ of the base × height.

Practise and Apply

4. Determine the volume of each cylinder. Express your answer to the nearest hundredth.

   a)
   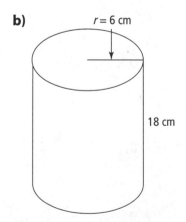
   r = 15 cm
   3 cm

   b)
   r = 6 cm
   18 cm

c)
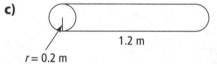
1.2 m
r = 0.2 m

5. Calculate the volume of each cylinder. Express your answer to the nearest hundredth.

   a) radius = 7 cm, height = 10 cm

   b) height = 3.2 m, radius = 1.2 m

6. Determine the volume of each cylinder.

a)

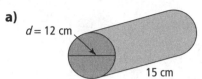

d = 12 cm

15 cm

b)

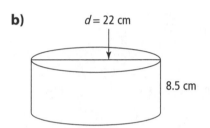

d = 22 cm

8.5 cm

c) diameter = 4 m
    height = 9 m

d) height = 32.5 cm
    diameter = 14 cm

7. Jade makes candles for the school craft sale. The candle mould she uses has a radius of 5 cm and a height of 6 cm.

a) How much wax does she need to fill the mould each time?

b) If she uses 628 cm³ of wax, how tall must the new candle mould be if the radius is 5 cm? Show your thinking.

8. How much soil will you need to fill the semi-circular planter? Express your answer to the closest thousandth.

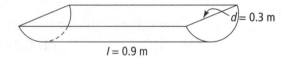

d = 0.3 m

l = 0.9 m

7.4 Solving Problems Involving Prisms and Cylinders

MathLinks 8, pages 268–275

Key Ideas Review

Unscramble the words to complete the sentences below.

1. **a)** There are many types of problems involving volumes of

   _____ and _____ .
   SIPSMR   SENYLCDRI

   b) You may need to decide which _____ to use.
                                          LUAFROM

   c) It may help to draw a _____ .
                                  RMAAGID

2. You may have to do more than one set of _____ .
                                              SONUATCLACLI

Practise and Apply

3. Patrick is packing his CDs because his family is moving. He has a box measuring 22 cm × 13 cm × 14 cm. Each CD measures 14 cm × 12.5 cm × 1 cm.

   a) Draw a sketch to show the best way for Patrick to pack the CDs.

   b) How many CDs will fit in the box? Show your thinking.

4. Kenu has a thermos of hot chocolate, which has a diameter of 10 cm and is 22 cm tall to the rim, not including the lid. The insulation is 1.5 cm thick.

   a) How much space is available for his hot chocolate? Express your answer to the closest hundredth.

   b) How much material is used for the insulation? Express your answer to the closest hundredth.

5. Cheyenne, Alisha, and Tia entered the ice sculpture contest at the winter carnival. This year contestants are given a block of ice to sculpt that measures 45 cm × 30 cm × 25 cm. Who has the least amount of ice shavings after sculpting objects from the block? Show your thinking.

Cheyenne

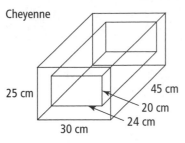

Tia

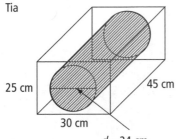

Alisha

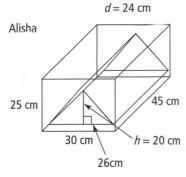

6. Steve is counting bead containers for inventory. Below is the bead container.

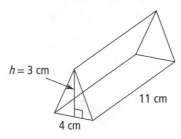

There are boxes filled with bead containers. Each box measures 20 cm × 11 cm × 12 cm.

a) Draw and label how you will pack the containers into each box.

b) What is the maximum number of bead containers each box will hold?

c) If there are three boxes, how many bead containers will Steve have to count?

Link It Together

1. Campers at Knotty Pines Day Camp will make All About Me bracelets to represent things about themselves. Each bracelet will have a number of beads from the four categories shown below.

Favourites   Characteristics   Hobbies   Goals

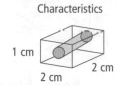
2 cm
d = 1 cm

1 cm
2 cm
2 cm

Hobbies
1 cm
1 cm

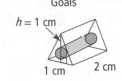
h = 1 cm
1 cm   2 cm

a) Create a design using a variety of the beads.

b) The beads are sold based on volume.
   • Use the measurements in the diagram.
   • The hole for the string has a diameter of 0.2 cm.
   Calculate the volume of each bead. Express your answers to the nearest hundredth.

c) What is the total volume of beads in your bracelet?

Vocabulary Link

Draw a line from the example or description in column A to the correct term in column B, then find each term in the word search.

A	B
1. the different position of an object formed by translating, rotating, or reflecting the object	a) area
	b) base of a prism
2. What figure does this visual show?	c) height
3. measured in square units	d) orientation
4. measured in cubic units	e) right cylinder
	f) right prism
5. In this visual, 8 mm represents the	g) volume
6.	
7. In this visual, the arrow points to the	

5 mm

8 mm

9 mm

?

H	K	H	J	X	R	M	O	E	Z	O	P	J	H	Y	Y	T	D	E	A
B	K	J	R	A	I	Q	H	I	O	K	I	K	T	A	G	N	U	B	A
N	M	F	V	H	G	B	U	Z	R	N	U	T	N	F	K	W	U	I	F
N	C	H	L	B	H	O	Q	H	I	E	J	V	Z	X	L	O	S	X	H
D	B	Z	I	A	T	E	M	S	E	V	D	V	G	V	K	A	T	N	L
I	D	Q	T	S	P	R	T	Q	N	G	B	G	J	L	F	G	U	Y	N
X	T	X	H	E	R	I	G	H	T	C	Y	L	I	N	D	E	R	C	P
B	M	A	E	O	I	D	F	F	A	W	P	B	F	F	A	J	P	E	R
G	T	X	A	F	S	C	A	E	T	Q	P	H	S	G	E	N	V	A	A
U	A	B	U	A	M	Y	A	L	I	D	L	E	K	J	S	H	N	R	J
Y	J	M	T	P	V	S	T	C	O	V	V	I	J	Y	R	O	S	B	Z
Z	Z	Z	B	R	Y	A	N	D	N	I	L	G	H	T	W	K	R	Y	R
C	J	E	A	I	Z	B	L	M	F	B	V	H	Q	V	R	D	C	Z	E
Q	P	G	C	S	E	C	T	R	M	P	O	T	R	V	D	T	N	L	G
W	A	W	M	M	X	L	W	D	Z	W	L	U	K	I	A	R	E	A	G
X	J	V	Z	K	Q	Q	J	D	D	W	U	W	B	T	Y	J	O	M	Z
E	Q	U	N	A	X	A	X	M	Y	Q	M	J	K	I	V	B	R	Z	F
O	D	P	P	K	G	V	I	V	U	O	E	T	H	B	J	E	F	Z	R

Get Ready

Represent Quantities With Integers

Integers include positive and negative whole numbers and zero.

An integer is any of the numbers
−3, −2, −1, 0, +1, +2, +3, ...

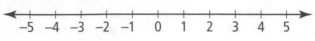

Integer chips are coloured disks that represent integers. A ⊕ represents +1;
and ⊖ represents −1.
• If you climb 5 steps, this amount can be represented by the integer +5.
• If you descend 10 steps, this amount can be represented by the integer −10.

1. Use an integer to represent each
   quantity. Explain your reasoning.

   a) an increase of 3%

   b) 20 m below sea level

2. Suppose you win a prize of $15. Use
   an integer to describe what happens

   a) from your point of view

   b) from the point of view of the
      person giving the prize

Adding Integers

A **zero pair** includes one ⊕ and one ⊖.
A zero pair represents zero.
Integer addition can be modelled using integer chips or diagrams.

zero pair

3. Use the diagram to complete each
   addition statement.

   a) ⊕⊕⊕⊕⊕⊕⊕
      ⊖⊖⊖⊖

      $(+7) + (-4) = \underline{+3}$

   b) ⊖⊖⊖⊖⊖⊖⊖⊖
      ⊕⊕⊕

      $(-8) + (+3) = \underline{-5}$

   c) ⊕ ⊕ ⊕ ⊕
      ⊖

      $(+4) + (-1) = \underline{+3}$

4. Use the diagram to complete each
   addition statement.

   a)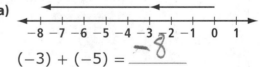

      $(-3) + (-5) = \underline{-8}$

   b)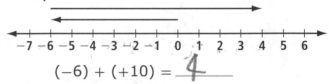

      $(-6) + (+10) = \underline{4}$

5. Complete each addition statement.

   a) $(+4) + (+5) = \underline{9}$

   b) $(-7) + (-7) = \underline{-14}$

   c) $(+6) + (-9) = \underline{-3}$

   d) $(-2) + (+8) = \underline{6}$

Subtracting Integers

Integer subtraction can be modelled using integer chips or diagrams.
Any integer subtraction can be completed by adding the opposite integer.
$(+5) - (-4) = (+5) + (+4)$
$\qquad = +9$

6. Use the diagrams to complete the subtraction statements.

a) $⊕⊕⊕⊕⊕⊕⊕ → ⊕⊕⊕⊕⊕⊕⊕ → ⊕⊕⊕$ $(+7) - (+4) = +3$

b) $⊖⊖⊖⊖⊖⊖ → ⊖⊖⊖⊖⊖⊖ → ⊖⊖⊖⊖$ $(-6) - (-2) = -4$

c) $⊖⊖ \_ ⊖⊖⊖⊖⊖⊖⊖⊖ \_ ⊖⊖⊖⊖⊖⊖⊖⊖ \_ ⊖⊖⊖⊖⊖⊖⊖⊖$ $(-2) - (+6) = -8$
$\quad ⊕⊕⊕⊕⊕⊕ \qquad ⊕⊕⊕⊕⊕⊕$

d) $⊖⊖⊖⊖ \_ ⊖⊖⊖⊖⊖⊖⊖ \_ ⊖⊖⊖⊖⊖⊖⊖ \_ ⊖⊖⊖$ $(-4) - (-7) = +3$
$\quad ⊕⊕⊕ \qquad ⊕⊕⊕ \qquad ⊕⊕⊕$

Order of Operations

The correct sequence of steps for a calculation follows the **order of operations** shown.

$8 \div 4 + (3 + 2) \times 6 - 7$ Do brackets first.
$= 8 \div 4 + 5 \times 6 - 7$ Multiply and divide from left to right.
$= 2 + 30 - 7$ Add and subtract from left to right.
$= 25$

7. Calculate. Show your thinking.

a) $8 + 6 \times 5 - 1$

$6 \times 5 = 30 + 8 = 38 - 1 = 37$

b) $3 \times (7 - 2) + 16 \div 4$

$7 - 2 = 5 \times 3 = 15 + 4 = 19$
$16 \div 4 = 4$

c) $24 \div 6 + 18 \div 2$

$24 \div 6 = 4 \quad 18 \div 2 = 9$
$4 + 9 = 13$

d) $(4 + 2) \div 6 + 6 \times 3 - 4$

$4 + 2 = 6 \div 6 = 1 \quad 6 \times 3 = 18$
$18 + 1 = 19 - 4 = 15$

8.1 Exploring Integer Multiplication

MathLinks 8, pages 286–292

Key Ideas Review

Choose from the terms below to complete #1.

~~insert~~   integer   ~~negative~~   positive   zero

1. a) To model the multiplication of an integer by a __positive__
   integer, you can __insert__ the appropriate integer chips. For
   example, $(+2) \times (-4) = -8$

   b) To model the multiplication of an integer by a __negative__
   integer, you can remove the appropriate integer chips from
   __zero__ pairs. For example, $(-2) \times (-5) = +10$

Practise and Apply

2. Write each repeated addition as a
   multiplication.

   a) $(+5) + (+5) + (+5) + (+5)$

   $+5 \times +4$

   b) $(-7) + (-7) + (-7)$

   $-7 \times +3$

   c) $(-3) + (-3) + (-3) + (-3) + (-3)$

   $-3 \times +5$

   d) $(+2) + (+2) + (+2)$

   $+2 \times +3$

3. Write each expression as a repeated
   addition.

   a) $(+4) \times (+1)$

   $1 + 1 + 1 + 1$

   b) $(+3) \times (-6)$

   $-6 + -6 + -6$

   c) $(+5) \times (-2)$

   $-2 + -2 + -2 + -2 + -2$

   d) $(+2) \times (+9)$

   $+9 + 9 ?$

4. What multiplication statement does each set of diagrams represent?

a)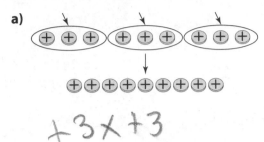

$+3 \times +3$

b)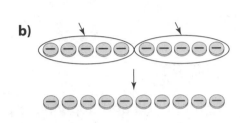

$-5 \times +2$

c)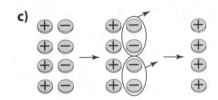

d)

5. Complete each multiplication statement. Show your thinking.

a) $(+2) \times (+8)$

b) $(+4) \times (-3)$

c) $(-1) \times (+8)$

d) $(-3) \times (-5)$

6. Use the multiplication of two integers to represent each situation. Then, determine the product and explain its meaning.

a) Serena mows her neighbour's lawn once a week. If she gets paid $6.00 each time, how much does she earn over eight weeks?

b) The temperature dropped 3 °C per hour. What was the total drop in temperature at the end of 12 hours?

8.2 Multiplying Integers

MathLinks 8, pages 293–299

Key Ideas Review

Choose from the terms below to complete #1 to #3. Then, complete the examples.

negative	number line	positive	same	sign

1. You can use a _____ to model multiplication of a

_____ integer by another integer.
For example, $(+4) \times (-1) = -4$ can be modelled as

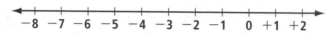

2. a) You can multiply two integers by multiplying the numerals and applying the

_____ rules below.

b) If both integers have the same sign, then the product is _____.

For example, $(-7) \times (-4) =$ _____ and $(+7) \times (+4) =$ _____

c) If the integers have different signs, then the product is _____.

For example, $(-7) \times (+4) =$ _____ and $(+7) \times (-4) =$ _____

3. It does not matter in what order you multiply 2 integers. You will get the

_____ answer. For example, $(+4) \times (-6) = -24$ or $(-6) \times (+4) =$ _____

Practise and Apply

4. Write the multiplication statement shown on each diagram.

a)

b)

```
+12
+10
 +8
 +6
 +4
 +2
  0
```

5. Draw a number line to determine each product.

a) $(+2) \times (-5)$

b) $(+4) \times (+4)$

6. Determine each product using the sign rules.

a) $(+7) \times (+6)$

b) $(+8) \times (-4)$

c) $(-5) \times (+9)$

d) $(-10) \times (-11)$

7. Estimate and then calculate.

a) $(+18) \times (+9)$

b) $(+32) \times (-15)$

c) $(-59) \times (+12)$

d) $(-98) \times (-18)$

8. Joshua spilled juice on his assignment. Fill in the integers that got smudged.

a) $(+10) \times (-4) =$ _____

b) $(-4) \times$ _____ $= -20$

c) _____ $\times (-8) = +16$

d) _____ $\times (-6) = -54$

e) $(+5) \times$ _____ $= +35$

9. An Internet provider offers a discount of $2.50 per month if a customer pays by automatic withdrawal.

a) How much will a customer save over two years?

b) How much will the Internet provider lose annually for each customer who makes this choice? Express this as an integer.

8.3 Exploring Integer Division

MathLinks 8, pages 300–305

Key Ideas Review

Draw a line from the model in Column A to the matching integer division statement in Column B.

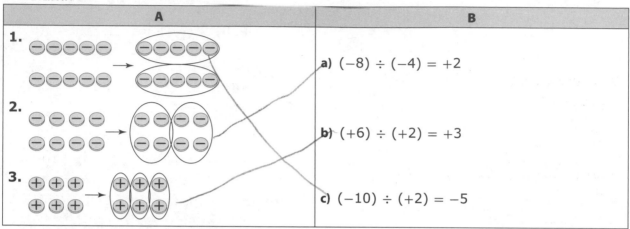

A	B
1.	a) $(-8) \div (-4) = +2$
2.	b) $(+6) \div (+2) = +3$
3.	c) $(-10) \div (+2) = -5$

Practise and Apply

4. Use the diagrams to complete each division statement.

   a) $(+12) \div (+6) =$ ___2___

   b) $(-15) \div (-3) =$ ___5___

   c) $(-8) \div (+4) =$ ___-2___

   d) $(+9) \div (+3) =$ ___3___

5. Use the diagram below each question to solve both statements.

   a) $(-10) \div (+2) =$ ___-5___
      $(-10) \div (-5) =$ ___2___

   b) $(-16) \div (-2) =$ ___8___
      $(-16) \div (+8) =$ ___-2___

   c) $(+6) \div (+3) =$ ___2___
      $(+6) \div (+2) =$ ___3___

6. Use the diagram to solve both statements.

$(-12) \div (+4) =$ ___-3___

$(-12) \div (-3) =$ ___4___

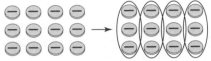

7. Draw a diagram to solve each question.

a) $(-14) \div (-7) =$ ___2___

b) $(+18) \div (+9) =$ ___2___

8. Examine this pattern.

$(-20) \div (-5) =$ _____

$(-15) \div (-5) =$ _____

$(-10) \div (-5) =$ _____

$(-5) \div (-5) =$ _____

$0 \div (-5) =$ _____

$(+5) \div (-5) =$ _____

$(+10) \div (-5) =$ _____

a) Use integer chips to complete the first four lines. Describe the pattern.

_____

_____

_____

b) Extend the pattern to determine the quotient $(+10) \div (-5)$.

9. Use the division of two integers to represent each situation and solve the problem.

a) Marcus scored 18 points during three games at his basketball tournament this weekend. If he scored the same number of points in each game, how many did he score per game?   6

b) Kellie played four games of hockey this weekend. She was on the ice when her opponents scored 20 goals. Her stats receive a -1 each time. What are her stats for each game this weekend?

$-20 \times 4 = -80$

20   -80

10. If the road's posted maximum speed is 100 km/h, how long will it take to drive 21 km? Use the division of two integers to represent this situation, then solve.

$100 \div 21 =$

11. Penelope gets a pay cheque of $750 every two weeks. If she works Monday to Friday, how much is earned each day? Use the division of two integers to represent this situation, then solve.

$750 \div 10 = 75$

8.4 Dividing Integers

MathLinks 8, pages 306–311

Key Ideas Review

Choose from the following terms to complete #1 and #2.

negative	number line	numerals	positive	sign	some

1. You can model _____ integer divisions on a

   _____ .

2. You can divide two integers by dividing the _____ and applying

   the _____ rules:

   a) The quotient of two integers with the same sign is _____ .

   b) The quotient of two integers with different signs is _____ .

Practise and Apply

3. Write two division statements that each diagram could represent.

   a)

   b)

4. Draw a number line to find each quotient.

   a) $(-9) \div (+3) =$ _____

   b) $(+10) \div (+5) =$ _____

   c) $(-12) \div (-6) =$ _____

   d) $(-15) \div (+5) =$ _____

5. Find each quotient.

   a) $(-22) \div (+2) =$ _____

   b) $(+18) \div (-6) =$ _____

6. Calculate and check.

a) $(-64) \div (-4) =$ _____

b) $(-52) \div (+52) =$ _____

c) $(+100) \div (-5) =$ _____

7. The product of two integers is +286. What is the other integer if one of them is −13? Show your thinking.

8. Tasha bought the same lunch at the school cafeteria every day last week. She spent a total of $15. How much did she spend each day? Show your thinking.

9. The new game system is out next week and Juan is short $60 to purchase one. He may borrow the rest of the money equally from his Mom, Dad, older sister, and aunt.

a) How much will Juan have to pay back to each person?

b) If Juan repays each person $5 a month, how many months will it take to pay off his debt?

10. Without calculating, circle the quotient with the highest value. Explain your reasoning.

$(-1972) \div (+35)$

$(-1972) \div (-35)$

$(+1972) \div (-35)$

_____

_____

11. A butterfly travels 6000 m in 30 min. How far does it travel per minute?

12. Danika is downloading a 1200 MB movie rental. The internet connection is running at 249 kB per second. How long will it take to get the movie? Show your thinking. Hint: 1 MB = 1000 kB

8.5 Applying Integer Operations

MathLinks 8, pages 312–317

Key Ideas Review

For #1 and #2, unscramble the letters to form a word that correctly completes the statement.

1. If you are solving a problem with integers, you need to decide which

   _____ to perform.
   NETIPRAOO

2. Some integer problems involve the _____ of
   REDOR

   _____.
   SAPTOOREIN

3. Put the statements in order according to the order of operations.

   _____ Multiply and divide, from left to right.

   _____ Add and subtract, from left to right.

   _____ Brackets.

Practise and Apply

4. Calculate using the order of operations. Show your thinking.

   a) $(+21) \div (-3) + (-2) \div (+1)$

   b) $(-15) \div [(-3) \times (-1)] + (+2)$

   c) $(-2) \times (-5) \div (-2) + (-7)$

   d) $[(-3) + (-8)] + (-1) \times (-4)$

5. Calculate.

   a) $(-7) + (-5) \times (+6) \div (-10)$

   b) $(-3) - (-4) \times (-10) - (-12)$

6. The chart shows the change in the attendance at games night.

Week	1	2	3	4	5	6
Attendance	+12	−4	+6	−10	+15	+1

   a) How many people were there the last week?

   b) Create an integer statement to show the change in attendance from week 1 to week 6.

Name: _____ **Date:** _____

7. Zelia loses seven points every three minutes that she doesn't make it to the next level on the video game.

   a) If she plays for 24 minutes without reaching the next level, how many points has she lost?

   b) If she played for three hours this month and never made it to the next level, how many points did she lose?

   c) If she lost 567 points, for how long did she play without reaching the next level?

8. The temperature change in the chicken egg incubator is recorded every hour (on a 24-h clock). The temperature at 8 a.m. was 35 °C.

Time	9	10	11	12	13	14	15	16
Temp(°C)	+2	+1	+1	−3	−1	+4	−1	−2

   a) When was the temperature highest? _____

      When was it lowest? _____

   b) Write an integer statement to represent the mean temperature change over the period shown.

9. Par 3 means that an expert golfer would take three strokes to complete the hole. The score indicates how many more (+) or fewer (−) strokes the player took to complete the hole. This is Paco's scorecard.

Hole	1	2	3	4	5	6	7	8	9
Par	3	3	3	3	3	3	3	3	3
Score	−1	+1	−2	Par	−2	+3	−1	+1	Par

   a) How many strokes did Paco take to complete the nine holes? Write an integer statement to represent the score, then solve.

   b) If his friend scored +1 on each hole, how many strokes did he take in total?

Link It Together

At a charity dinner, money was raised by selling draw tickets for $100 each. There were 290 tickets sold. Some of the money was then given away as nine draw prizes of $1000 each. Write an integer statement for each of the following scenarios, and then solve.

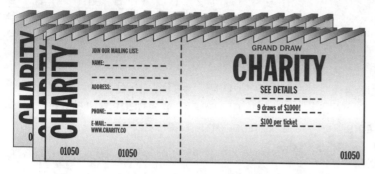

1. How much money remained for the charity after the prizes were awarded?

2. At Keeley's table there were seven other guests. Each person said they would share their winnings minus the price of the ticket equally with everyone else at the table. Keeley won one of the $1000 draws. How much did each person at the table receive from her winnings?

3. Keeley's Dad bought a table of tickets for his employees (seven tickets, plus one for himself). Two employees' tickets won. How much money did the table give to the charity? Explain.

Vocabulary Link

Use the clues to identify the key words from Chapter 8. Then, write them in the crossword puzzle blank.

Across

4. The second integer order of operation you perform is multiplying and dividing in

_____ from left to right.

5. The third integer order of operation is adding and subtracting, in order, from

_____ _____ _____.

Down

1. The _____ _____ include:

- the product or quotient of two integers with the same sign is positive
- the product or quotient of two integers with different signs is negative

2. What do you do first in the order of operations? _____.

3. This visual shows a(n) _____ _____.

6. Any of the numbers –2, –1, 0, +1, +2, … is a(n) _____.

Name: _____ **Date:** _____

Describe Patterns in Words

Patterns can be described using words. When you describe a pattern, tell what it is, where it starts, and how it changes.
- The pattern of letters *a, c, e, ...* can be described as letters of the alphabet beginning with *a*, and skipping one letter each time or increasing by two letters.
- The number pattern 6, 9, 12, ... can be described as whole numbers that begin with 6, and increase by 3 or are multiples of 3.

1. Describe each pattern in words.

   a) *b, e, h, ...*

   Going up by 3

   b) 9, 4, –1, ...

   Subtracting by 5

Show Patterns in a Table

A café has small tables that seat four people. Small tables can be moved together to seat larger groups as shown.

The information from this pattern can be shown in a table.

Number of Tables	1	2	3
Number of Chairs	4	6	8

You can describe the pattern as "the number of chairs begins at 4 and increases by 2 each time you add a table."

2. For each pattern, make a table of values and then describe the pattern.

   a)

# table	how many
1	4
2	7
3	10

   Going up by 3

   b)

table #	how many
1	4
2	6
3	8

   Going up by 2

Describe Patterns Using an Expression

There are three algae eaters and some guppies in a fish tank. If the number of guppies is represented by the **variable** g, the total number of fish in the tank can be expressed as g + 3.

3. Write an expression for each scenario. Tell what your variable represents.

   a) Shay has five boxes of pencils. Each box has the same number of pencils. How many pencils does he have in total?

b) A Winnipeg warehouse has 12 shipping cartons of DVDs. Each carton has the same number of DVDs. The cartons will be sent to four different cities. How many DVDs will go to each city?

$$12 \div 4 = 3$$

3 DVDs to each city

Use a Coordinate Grid

Points on a coordinate grid are described using **ordered pairs** written as (x, y).

Point E can be described using the ordered pair (3, 1).

- The first coordinate, or **x-coordinate**, is the horizontal distance of point E from the y-axis.
- The second coordinate, or **y-coordinate**, is the vertical distance of point E from the x-axis. You can locate points by counting from the origin (0, 0).

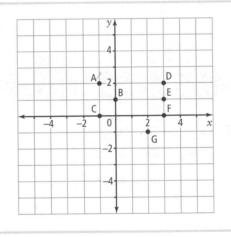

4. Enter each point from the above coordinate grid in the table below.

Point	E	C	G	D	A	B	F
x	3	−1	2	3	−1	0	0
y	1	0	−1	2	2	1	0

9.1 Analysing Graphs of Linear Relations

MathLinks 8, **pages 332–341**

Key Ideas Review

Use the graph at right to answer questions #1 to #4.

1. Complete a table of values for the graph.

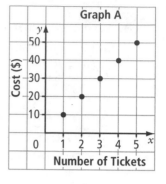

Graph A

Cost ($) vs *Number of Tickets*

2. Circle the three factors that should be included to describe the pattern on a graph.

   a) where it starts   **b)** how it changes   **c)** slope of the line

   d) *x*-axis and *y*-axis titles   **e)** what it relates to

3. Does the graph above show a linear relation? How do you know?

   _____

   _____

4. Does it make sense to have values between those on the graph? Explain.

   _____

   _____

Practise and Apply

5. Complete the sentences to describe the graph below.

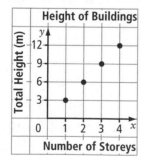

Height of Buildings

Total Height (m) vs Number of Storeys

   a) The height of a one-storey building is _____ m, a _____-storey building is 6 m high, a three-storey building is _____ m, ...

   b) The points appear to lie in a

   _____. The line

   shows a _____ relation.

   c) The graph shows that to move from one point to the next, you go _____ unit horizontally, and _____ units vertically.

   d) Complete the table of values for this graph.

	1	2	3	4		10
	3				15	

6. The graph shows the cost of gasoline based on the volume of gas.

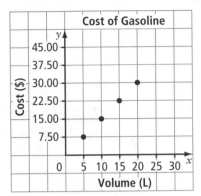

a) Does the graph show a linear relation? Explain.

_____

_____

_____

b) The graph shows that for every five units horizontally, you go

_____ units vertically.

c) Complete the table of values from the graph.

Volume (L)	Cost ($)
5	7.50

d) Would it be reasonable to include a point for 7 L? Explain.

_____

_____

_____

e) What is the cost of gasoline per litre?

f) If the graph continued, what would be the cost of

25 L?

30 L?

7. The graph shows the maximum number of customers based on the number of tables in the restaurant.

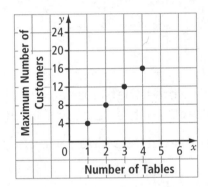

a) Title the graph.

b) Describe the patterns on the graph. Does the graph show a linear relation?

_____

_____

_____

c) Complete the table of values for the graph.

	1			4	5	6
	4	8				

9.2 Patterns in a Table of Values

MathLinks 8, pages 342–351

Key Ideas Review

Match the terms in column B to a representation of a linear relation in column A.

A	B
1. $(l, 3l)$	**a)** table of values
2. The cost in dollars is $3l$, where l is the length in metres.	**b)** graph
3. table: l = 0, 1, 2, 3; c = 0, 3, 6, 9	**c)** words
4. The cost in dollars is three times the length in metres.	**d)** ordered pair
5. graph	**e)** expression

3.

l	0	1	2	3
c	0	3	6	9

6. Circle the words that correctly complete each statement.
You can tell that the relationship in #3 is linear because

- Each consecutive value for c changes by (the same/a different) amount.
- Each consecutive value for l changes by (the same/a different) amount.

Practise and Apply

7. Graph the ordered pairs in the table of values.

l	m
2	7
4	9
6	11
8	13

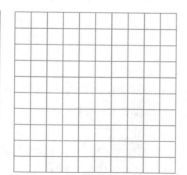

8. Circle the table(s) of values that show a linear relation. Explain your answer.

a)

l	m
2	7
4	9
6	11
8	13

b)

a	b
3	8
6	12
9	15
12	19

_____

_____

_____

9. The table of values represents a linear relation.

x	0	1	2	3	4	5
d	0	3	6	9	12	15

a) Graph the ordered pairs.

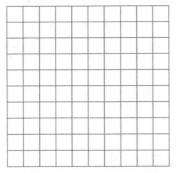

b) What is the difference in value for consecutive x-values?

c) What is the difference in value for consecutive d-values?

d) The d-value is _____ times the x-value.

e) Write an expression for d in terms of x.

10. For what number of hours is it cheaper to rent by the day rather than by the hour? Show your work.

$20/h
$80/day
+ $10 insurance

11. The following pattern of triangles continues. The side of each triangle is 2 cm.

a) Complete the table of values to show the relationship between the number of triangles and the perimeter of each figure.

Number of Triangles	1	2	3	4
Perimeter (cm)	6	8		

b) Draw a graph from the table of values.

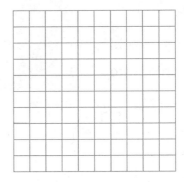

c) Describe the relationship shown on the graph.

_____

_____

_____

d) What is an expression for the perimeter in terms of the number of triangles? Explain what the variables mean.

e) If the pattern continues, what is the perimeter when there are 30 triangles? Show your thinking.

9.3 Linear Relationships

MathLinks 8, pages 352–359

Key Ideas Review

For #1 and #2, unscramble the letters to form a word that correctly completes the statement.

1. a) You can graph a linear _____ represented by

   a(n) _____ or a(n) _____ .

   AEILNORT

   AFLMORU   AEIUNOQT

   b) First, make a table of _____ .

   AELUVS

   Check that the values in the table are _____ .

   AABEELNORS

   c) Then, graph using the _____ pairs in the table.

   EEDDORR

t	d
0	0
1	40
2	80
3	120
4	160
5	200

2. Whenever possible, choose variables that are meaningful.

   For example, *d* for _____ and *t*

   AECDISTN

   for _____ .

   EITM

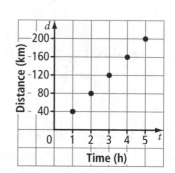

Practise and Apply

3. The amount of water used by a garden hose can be represented as $V = 20t$, where *V* is the volume of water in litres, and *t* is the time in minutes.

   a) Complete the table of values.

t	V
0	0
1	20
3	
4	
5	

   b) Graph the ordered pairs.

   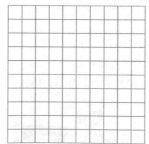

   c) Is it reasonable to have points between the ones on the graph? Explain.

   _____

   _____

   _____

4. The use of computers is free in most libraries, but most libraries charge for using the printer. The cost of printing can be represented by $C = 15p$, where C is the cost in cents, and p is the number of pages printed.

a) Complete the table of values.

p	0	1	2	3	4	5
C						

b) Graph the ordered pairs.

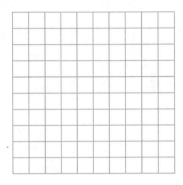

c) Is it reasonable to have points between the ones on the graph? Explain.

_____

_____

_____

5. Evaluate each equation using the given value. Show your thinking.

a) $y = 3x - 1$ when $x = 5$

b) $y = 4x + 1$ when $x = -3$

c) $y = -x$ when $x = -4$

6. Complete the table of values for each equation using $x = -2, -1, 0, 1, 2$.

a) $y = 4x + 1$

x					
y					

b) $y = -5x$

x					
y					

c) $y = 3 - x$

x					
y					

7. This graph represents part of the linear relation $y = -x + 4$.

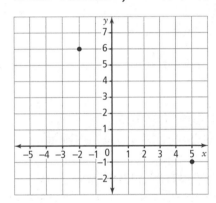

a) What are the coordinates for the point that lies on the y-axis?

b) What is the y-coordinate when $x = 3$?

c) For the point $(-10, y)$, what is the value of y?

Link It Together

A scuba diver is 60 metres underwater and rises at a rate of 20 metres every minute.

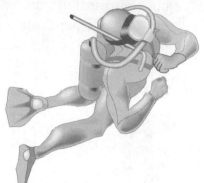

1. Make a table of values to show the diver's rise to the surface.

2. a) Plot the ordered pairs on the graph.

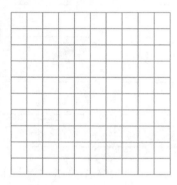

   b) Title the graph.

   c) Describe the pattern on the graph.

_____

_____

3. a) What is the difference between consecutive values in the chart?

_____

   b) Write an expression for this relationship. Explain what each part of the expression means.

4. Is it reasonable to extend the graph above 0 metres? Explain.

_____

5. Does the graph show a linear relationship? Explain.

_____

Vocabulary Link

Draw a line from the example in column A to the correct term in column B. Then, find each term in the word search.

A	B
1. $C = \pi d$, where C is the circumference and d is the diameter of a circle. **2.** 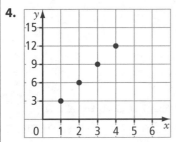 **3.** A pattern formed by two sets of numbers. **4.** **5.** $y = 4x$ **6.** $6c - 2$ **7.** An unknown number, c.	**a)** equation **b)** expression **c)** formula **d)** linear relation **e)** relationship **f)** table of values **g)** variable

For item 2:

Hieght (m)	0	150	300	450	600	750
Temperature (°C)	20					

```
N  I  V  B  V  M  J  H  A  G  V  Y  U  U  R  A  T  E  V  G
T  R  S  N  W  L  U  L  Z  Y  X  R  K  Z  G  E  E  I  O  Z
E  A  U  E  V  H  U  T  E  C  F  S  F  O  F  Z  Q  R  Z  G
I  L  B  Q  R  M  D  X  L  U  C  F  S  N  N  L  U  S  P  T
Z  Y  P  L  R  O  U  E  E  R  Q  L  W  U  Z  Q  A  O  I  U
E  Q  D  O  E  G  M  L  T  K  N  F  C  E  V  W  T  D  L  M
X  V  F  U  T  O  B  P  B  W  M  K  Q  I  T  F  I  L  U  S
P  M  Y  I  C  A  F  B  J  S  U  Z  L  E  N  Y  O  V  U  V
R  M  G  Z  I  W  E  V  Y  H  O  W  F  J  B  D  N  L  H  C
E  A  L  R  E  B  H  K  A  T  V  K  S  O  C  V  E  K  G  Z
S  F  A  T  Q  X  K  J  P  L  Y  R  M  A  U  A  F  F  K  U
S  V  Z  O  C  W  K  F  C  S  U  C  V  E  J  P  G  N  L  V
I  A  D  N  E  I  L  Q  D  I  X  E  S  N  E  N  X  U  G  W
O  S  E  V  L  E  R  N  U  W  X  B  S  D  D  S  G  B  S  B
N  J  L  I  N  E  A  R  R  E  L  A  T  I  O  N  K  C  R  E
W  T  J  R  E  L  A  T  I  O  N  S  H  I  P  Z  F  P  O  E
M  T  J  K  M  N  G  L  Y  P  S  H  Q  M  K  S  O  T  X  J
A  N  T  N  P  G  W  W  U  N  L  T  M  N  S  W  R  Z  E  D
```

Name: _____ **Date:** _____

Substituting Values Into Equations

When you are substituting values into equations, make sure you use the correct order of operations:
- brackets first
- multiply and divide in order from left to right
- add and subtract in order from left to right

Determine the value of y when substituting $x = 7$ into the following equation.

$y = 2(x - 3) + 5$
$y = 2(7 - 3) + 5$ Brackets.
$y = 2(4) + 5$ Multiply.
$y = 8 + 5$ Add.
$y = 13$

1. Determine the value of y in each equation when $d = 6$.

   a) $y = (3d + 4) \div 2 + 8$

   b) $y = (3 + d - 7) \times 4d + 5$

2. Calculate the surface area of a rectangular prism using the formula $SA = 2(bh + bl + hl)$, where $b = 5$ cm, $h = 11$ cm, $l = 12$ cm.

Modelling and Solving One-Step Equations

To solve a problem, you sometimes need to translate words into equations. For example, "the sum of 4 and another number is 12" can be modelled by the equation $4 + x = 12$.
The equation can now be solved.

$x + 4 = 12$
$x + 4 - 4 = 12 - 4$ Subtract 4 from both sides of the equation.
$x = 8$

3. Model each situation with an algebraic equation.

   a) seven more than a number, p, is twelve

   b) three less than a number, x, is eleven

   c) four times a number, s, is twenty-eight

   d) when a number, k, is divided by six, the result is nine

4. Develop and solve an algebraic equation for each question.

a) If Jim's height increased by 13 cm over the past year and he is now 152 cm, how tall was he a year ago?

b) Ayisha worked twice as long on a math project as Harpreet did. If Ayisha worked for 50 min on the project, how long did Harpreet work on it?

Solving Two-Step Equations

To solve a two-step problem of the form $ax + b = c$, you need to isolate the variable on one side of the equal sign. When undoing the operations performed on the variable, follow the reverse order of operations:
- Subtract and add in order from left to right.
- Multiply and divide in order from left to right.

Solve $6x + 7 = 25$

$6x + 7 - 7 = 25 - 7$ Subtract 7 from both sides of the equation.

$6x = 18$

$\dfrac{6x}{6} = \dfrac{18}{6}$ Divide both sides of the equation by 6.

$x = 3$

Check: Left Side $= 6x + 7$ Right Side $= 25$

$= 6(3) + 7$

$= 18 + 7$

$= 25$

Left Side $=$ Right Side

The solution is correct.

5. For each equation, circle the first operation you undo and underline the second operation you undo.

a) $2n + 4 = 18$ **b)** $3x + 5 = 17$

c) $8y - 70 = 94$ **d)** $27 = 7q + 6$

6. Solve each equation. Check your solution.

a) $9 + 5j = 49$

b) $4t + 2 = 14$

10.1 Modelling and Solving One-Step Equations: $ax = b$, $\dfrac{x}{a} = b$

MathLinks 8, pages 370–379

Key Ideas Review

Match each method in column A with an example from column B.

A	B
1. Solve by inspection. _____ **2.** Model the equation using concrete materials, and then balance it. _____ **3.** Perform the opposite operation on both sides of the equal sign. _____ **4.** Check your solution by modelling or substitution. _____	**a)** $-3a = 12$ $\dfrac{-3a}{-3} = \dfrac{12}{-3}$ $a = -4$ **b)** Ask yourself, "What number results from dividing −12 by −3?" **c)** $\boxed{-a} = \boxed{-1}\,\boxed{-1}\,\boxed{-1}\,\boxed{-1}$ $\boxed{-a} = \boxed{-1}\,\boxed{-1}\,\boxed{-1}\,\boxed{-1}$ $\boxed{-a} = \boxed{-1}\,\boxed{-1}\,\boxed{-1}\,\boxed{-1}$ **d)** Left Side = $-3a$ Right Side = 12 $= -3(-4)$ $= 12$ Left Side = Right Side

Practise and Apply

5. Write the equation modelled by the diagrams.

a) $\boxed{r} \; \boxed{r} = \boxed{+1}\,\boxed{+1}\,\boxed{+1}\,\boxed{+1}\; / \;\boxed{+1}\,\boxed{+1}\,\boxed{+1}\,\boxed{+1}$

b) $\boxed{-s}\;\boxed{-s}\;\boxed{-s} = \boxed{+1}\,\boxed{+1}\,\boxed{+1}\;/\;\boxed{+1}\,\boxed{+1}\,\boxed{+1}\;/\;\boxed{+1}\,\boxed{+1}\,\boxed{+1}$

c) $\dfrac{x}{4}$ = $\boxed{+1}\,\boxed{+1}\;/\;\boxed{+1}\,\boxed{+1}$

d) $\boxed{-m}\;\boxed{-m}\;\boxed{-m}\;\boxed{-m} = \boxed{-1}\,\boxed{-1}\,\boxed{-1}\,\boxed{-1}\;/\;\boxed{-1}\,\boxed{-1}\,\boxed{-1}\,\boxed{-1}\;/\;\boxed{-1}\,\boxed{-1}\,\boxed{-1}\,\boxed{-1}\;/\;\boxed{-1}\,\boxed{-1}\,\boxed{-1}\,\boxed{-1}$

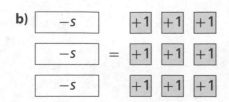

6. Solve by inspection.

a) $-7g = 56$ b) $-81 = 9p$

c) $\frac{-n}{5} = -6$ d) $-7 = \frac{b}{3}$

7. Use models to solve each equation. Show your thinking.

a) $-9 = 3t$

b) $\frac{b}{4} = -2$

8. By what number would you divide both sides of the equation to solve it?

a) $14 = -7z$ b) $-8g = -64$

9. Solve each equation using the opposite operation. Check your answer.

a) $5a = -25$

b) $-63 = -7k$

10. By what number would you multiply both sides of the equation to solve it?

a) $\frac{x}{5} = -3$ b) $-9 = \frac{d}{-4}$

11. Show whether $y = 18$ is the solution to each equation.

a) $72 = \frac{y}{-4}$ b) $-9 = -2y$

c) $-3 = \frac{y}{-6}$ d) $2y = 36$

12. The cost of an adult ticket for a concert is three times the cost of a child's ticket. If an adult ticket costs $48 what is the cost for a child's ticket?

a) Write an equation to represent this problem. What does your variable represent?

b) Solve the equation. Verify your answer.

13. An LED light bulb lasts 50 times longer than an incandescent light bulb.

a) Write an equation to represent this situation.

b) If an incandescent light bulb lasts 1000 hours, how long does an LED light bulb last? Show your thinking.

10.2 Modelling and Solving Two-Step Equations: $ax + b = c$

MathLinks 8, pages 380–387

Key Ideas Review

Circle the correct response to complete each statement.

1. To solve an equation, (isolate/reverse) the variable on one side of the equal sign.

2. When undoing the operations performed on the variable, (reverse/follow) the order of operations.

3. Check your solution by (substitution/switching) or drawing a diagram.

4. In the visuals used in this chapter, a white box or rectangle represents a (negative/positive) integer.

5. In the visuals used in this chapter, a grey box or rectangle represents a (negative/positive) integer.

Practise and Apply

6. Write and solve each equation modelled below. Check your solution.

   a)
x	+1		+1	+1	+1
x	+1	=	+1	+1	+1
x			+1	+1	

   b)
x		=	−1	−1
x		=	−1	−1
x		=	−1	−1

   c)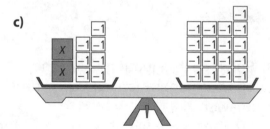

7. Circle the first operation you should undo to solve each equation. Underline the second operation you should undo.

   a) $5 + 3x = -7$ b) $4r - 6 = 14$

   c) $13 = -6y - 11$ d) $-89 = 9t - 26$

8. Solve the equation. Check your solution.

  a) $2x + 5 = 11$

  b) $4p + 3 = 19$

  c) $-25 = -6a - 43$

  d) $15 = -11d - 18$

9. The Hornets won 19 games. This is 5 less than 4 times the number of games the Vampires won.

  a) Let v represent the Vampires' wins. What equation models this situation? Explain your thinking.

  _____

  _____

  _____

  b) How many games did the Vampires win?

10. Show whether $x = 5$ is the solution to each equation.

  a) $4x + 6 = -20$ **b)** $-5 - 2x = -15$

  c) $8x - 4 = 36$ **d)** $13x + 12 = 77$

11. The length of a square's side is 10 cm. This square's perimeter is 7 cm more than the perimeter of an equilateral triangle.

  a) Let s represent the length of one side of the triangle. What equation models this situation?

  b) Solve the equation to find the length of the triangle's sides. Verify your answer.

12. A chalet rents for $150 plus $72 per person for a weekend.

  a) Write an equation to model this situation.

  b) How much will it cost 16 people to rent the chalet for one night?

  c) If the group budgets $1950 for the chalet rental, how many people can stay for the weekend?

10.3 Modelling and Solving Two-Step Equations:

$$\frac{x}{a} + b = c$$

MathLinks 8, pages 388–393

Key Ideas Review

Choose from the following terms to complete #1.

add	divide	isolate	reverse	substituting	value

1. **a)** To solve an equation, _____ the variable on one side of the equal sign.

   b) When undoing the operations performed on the variable, follow the

   _____ order of operations.

   • subtract and/or _____

   • multiply and/or _____

   c) One method you can use to check your answer is _____ it back into the equation. Both sides should have the same

   _____.

Practise and Apply

2. Solve the equation modelled by each diagram. Check your solution.

   a)
   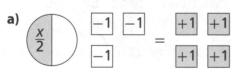

   b)

3. Draw a model for each equation, and then solve. Verify your answer.

   a) $\frac{x}{-5} + 6 = 4$ **b)** $-5 + \frac{y}{3} = -3$

   c) $2 = 14 + \frac{n}{3}$ **d)** $16 = 9 + \frac{c}{-7}$

4. What are the first and second operations you should perform to solve each equation?

a) $\frac{f}{6} + 2 = -4$ **b)** $\frac{r}{-3} - 6 = 7$

_____

_____

c) $12 = 7 + \frac{z}{-5}$ **d)** $\frac{k}{11} - 12 = 6$

_____

_____

5. Solve each equation.

a) $\frac{d}{-4} - 5 = -3$ **b)** $4 + \frac{n}{2} = 20$

c) $-6 = \frac{b}{-3} + 11$ **d)** $\frac{p}{13} - 2 = -3$

6. Show whether $h = 12$ is the solution to each equation.

a) $-6 = \frac{h}{-4} - 3$ **b)** $5 = 11 - \frac{h}{2}$

c) $\frac{-h}{12} + 8 = 9$ **d)** $\frac{h}{3} - 1 = 3$

7. Rick saved $400 to buy a pair of skis. On Rick's birthday, his brother Jon gave him one eighth of his savings. Including the gift, Rick then had $475. Let j represents Jon's total savings. Write and solve an equation to determine Jon's savings before he gave Rick the gift.

8. In the following formula, f is the speed that a peregrine falcon can dive in km/h, and c is the speed of a cheetah in km/h: $\frac{f}{5} + 30 = c$. If the top speed of a cheetah is 100 km/h, how fast can a peregrine falcon dive? Show your thinking.

9. The discounted price of an airplane ticket is one third of the regular price, plus $137 in taxes and airport fees.

a) Write an equation to represent this situation.

b) If the discount ticket to Paris costs $349, what is the regular price?

c) If the regular ticket price to Vancouver is $699, what will a discount ticket cost?

10.4 Modelling and Solving Two-Step Equations: $a(x + b) = c$

MathLinks 8, pages 394–399

Key Ideas Review

For #1 to #4, unscramble the letters to form a word that correctly completes the statement.

1. To solve an equation, _____ the variable on one side of the equal sign.
   OITSLAE

2. When _____ the operations performed on the variable, use
   DIUONNG
   _____ operations.
   PTIOOPES

3. Solve equations in the form $a(x + b) = c$ by _____ first, or by
   DDGIIINV
   using the _____ property.
   BDEIIISRTTUV

4. Check your _____ by substituting it back into the equation.
   AENRSW
   Both _____ should have the same value.
   EIDSS

Practise and Apply

5. Solve the equation modelled by each diagram. Check your solution.

   a)
x	-1	-1		$+1$	$+1$	$+1$	$+1$
x	-1	-1	=	$+1$	$+1$	$+1$	$+1$

   b)
$+1$	$+1$	$+1$		x	-1	-1	-1	-1
$+1$	$+1$	$+1$	=	x	-1	-1	-1	-1
$+1$	$+1$	$+1$		x	-1	-1	-1	-1

   c)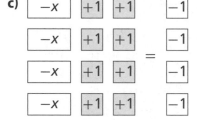

   d)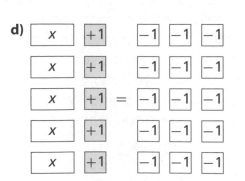

6. Model and then solve each equation. Check your solution.

   a) $4(t - 5) = 8$

   b) $5(r + 7) = -55$

7. Solve each equation. Check your answer.

   a) $-3(x - 8) = 12$

   b) $600 = 4(s + 4)$

   c) $2(x - 3) = 6$

8. Beth would like to put a 2-m wide grass border around a square garden that has a perimeter of 44 m.

   a) What equation models this situation?

   b) If she wants a fence around the outside of the grass border, what length of fencing will she have to buy?

9. Aaron is driving to his friend's place 180 km away. If he can average a speed that is 5 km/h more than his current speed and then triple that, he will arrive in two hours.

   a) Using s for his current speed, what equation models this situation?

   b) Determine Aaron's speed.

Link It Together

Many items depreciate or lose value over time. As a car gets older, its value automatically depreciates a certain amount each year. The relationship between a car's age and its value is linear. Several equations are used to calculate a car's depreciation.

1. Write an equation to represent each of the following depreciation methods. Identify your variables.

   a) The depreciation is the number of years owned times 1000.

   b) The depreciation is the age of the car times one tenth the cost of the car.

   c) The depreciation is the cost of the car minus $2750 and then times one fiftieth the age of the car.

2. Calculate the depreciation of a $20 000 car after three years, using each of the equations in #1. Show your thinking.

3. Complete the table using the equation from #1b). Show your thinking.

Age of Car (Yr)	Value of Car ($)
0	30 000
1	
2	
5	
8	
10	

Vocabulary Link

Use the clues to identify the key words from Chapter 10. Then, write them in the crossword puzzle blank.

Across

3. In −84 = 12*d*, _____ 12*d* by dividing both sides of the equation by 12.

7. In 5*d* + 4 = 39, 5 is the _____ _____.

8. When solving an equation such as 6*a* − 4 = 26, you need to use the

_____ _____ to isolate the variable.

9. In the equation $\frac{m}{7}$ = 6, *m* is the _____.

Down

1. In the equation 5*w* + 1 = *t*, 1 is a _____.

2. 5(*s* + 2) = 5*s* + 10 uses the _____ property.

4. A mathematical statement with two expressions that have the same value is

called a(n) _____.

5. When graphed, a _____ equation such as $d = \frac{c}{2}$ results in points along a straight line.

6. When solving 6*a* = 72, you need to _____ the variable.

Get Ready

Fractions, Decimals, and Percents

To convert a fraction to a percent, convert the fraction to a decimal number by dividing the numerator by the denominator. Then, multiply the decimal by 100 and add a percent symbol.

$$\frac{4}{9} = 0.444\,44...$$
$$= 0.444\,44... \times 100\%$$
$$= 44.\overline{4}\%$$

Use a bar over the repeating part of a repeating decimal.

1. Complete the following table.

	Fraction	Decimal	Percent
a)	$\frac{4}{5}$		
b)		0.666666...	
c)	$\frac{4}{11}$		
d)			$33.\overline{3}\%$

Probability

The probability of an event is a measure of the likelihood that it will occur. The probability of an impossible event is 0 or 0%. The probability of a certain event is 1 or 100%.

A coin is flipped. What is the probability that it lands heads up, $P(H)$? Write your answer as a fraction, a decimal, and a percent.

$$P(H) = \frac{\text{favourable outcomes}}{\text{possible outcomes}}$$
$$= \frac{1}{2}$$

The probability of heads is $\frac{1}{2}$, 0.5, or 50%.

2. The spinner is spun once. What is the probability of spinning 2, $P(2)$? Write the answer as a fraction, a decimal, and a percent.

Using Tables and Tree Diagrams

Tables and tree diagrams are common ways to organize outcomes. A coin is flipped and a spinner is spun. Below is the sample space.

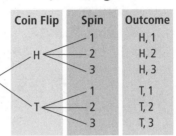

Table

Coin	Spinner		
	1	**2**	**3**
Heads (H)	H, 1	H, 2	H, 3
Tails (T)	T, 1	T, 2	T, 3

Tree Diagram

Coin Flip	Spin	Outcome
H	1	H, 1
	2	H, 2
	3	H, 3
T	1	T, 1
	2	T, 2
	3	T, 3

There are 6 possible outcomes: (H, 1), (H, 2), (H, 3), (T, 1), (T, 2), (T, 3).

P(T, 3) is $\frac{1}{6}$, $0.1\overline{6}$, or $16.\overline{6}\%$.

3. a) Create a table to show the sample space for the spinner and the fair six-sided die.

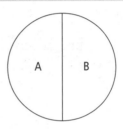 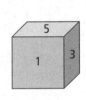

b) List the sample space.

c) What is P(A, < 5)?

Multiplying Fractions

You can use paper folding to multiply proper fractions.

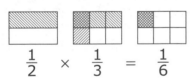

$$\frac{1}{2} \times \frac{1}{3} = \frac{1}{6}$$

To multiply fractions without a diagram, multiply the numerators and multiply the denominators.

$$\frac{1}{2} \times \frac{1}{3} = \frac{1 \times 1}{2 \times 3} = \frac{1}{6}$$

4. What multiplication statement does the diagram represent?

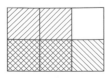

5. Multiply. Show your answer in lowest terms.

$$\frac{3}{5} \times \frac{5}{6}$$

11.1 Determining Probabilities Using Tree Diagrams and Tables

MathLinks 8, pages 410–418

Key Ideas Review

Match each statement in column A to a term in column B.

A	B
1. Determined from tree diagrams and tables. ___d___	a) probability
2. The probability of A then B occurring. ___e___	b) tree diagrams
3. The number of favourable outcomes divided by the total number of possible outcomes. ___a___	c) P(A, B)
4. The probability both A and B occurring. ___c___	d) probabilities
5. Used to show sample space for a probability experiment. ___b___	e) P(A then B)

Practise and Apply

6. The following tree diagram shows the sample space for flipping a coin and rolling a six-sided die. Fill in the outcome column.

Coin Flip	Spin	Outcome
Heads	1 2 3 4 5 6	h1, h2, h3, h4, h5, h6
Tails	1 2 3 4 5 6	t1, t2, t3, t4, t5, t6

a) What is P(H, 6)?

$\frac{1}{12}$ or 0.083 or 8.3%

b) What is P(T, odd number)?

$\frac{3}{12} = \frac{1}{4}$ or 0.25 or 25%

c) What is P(H, 7)?

$\frac{1}{10}$ or 0.083 or 8.3%

7. A four-sided die labelled 1, 2, 3, and 4 is rolled and a spinner labelled 3, 6, and 9 is spun.

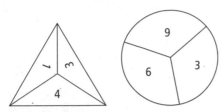

a) Create a table to show the sample space.

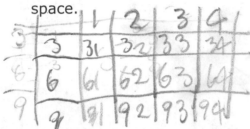

	1	2	3	4
3	31	32	33	34
6	61	62	63	64
9	91	92	93	94

b) What is P(sum even number)?

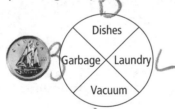

$\frac{6}{12}$ or $b. 42$ or 42%

8. Each week Sam (H) and Lacy (T) choose chores by flipping a coin and spinning a spinner.

a) Draw a tree diagram to show the sample space.

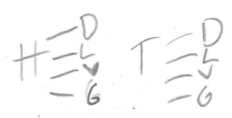

b) What is the probability that Sam will have to do dishes this week?

$\frac{1}{8}$

9. In this card game there are two identical sets of six cards. You pick up a card from each set. The idea of the game is to make a sum of 10.

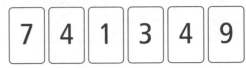

a) Create a table to show all the combinations.

b) What is $P(3, 3)$?

10. Trey chooses his outfits by spinning this spinner twice. The first spin is for the colour of pants and the second spin is for the colour of shirt.

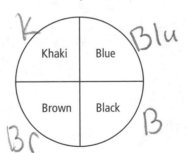

a) Show the sample space.

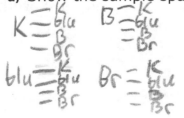

b) What is P(same colour)?

$\frac{4}{16}$

11.2 Outcomes of Independent Events

MathLinks 8, pages 419–425

Key Ideas Review

Use the diagrams to fill in the blanks for #1.

1. Name the methods shown that can be used to determine the possible number of outcomes.

	1	2	3	4
Blue	B, 1	B, 2	B, 3	B, 4
Red	R, 1	R, 2	R, 3	R, 4

   $2 \times 4 = 8$

   a) _____

   b) _____

   c) _____

Practise and Apply

2. Christine is making her lunch. She can choose strawberry, peach, or raspberry yogurt and an apple, an orange, grapes, or a banana. She picks one yogurt and one piece of fruit.

   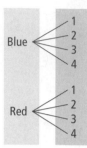

   a) Draw a tree diagram to show the sample space.

   b) How many possible outcomes are there?

   c) Check your answer using multiplication.

3. A new game uses the following two spinners.

   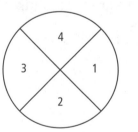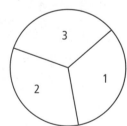

   a) Use multiplication to determine the total number of possible outcomes.

   b) Check your answer using another method.

4. Aira is ordering pizza for her birthday party. There are three choices for crusts (thin, regular, stuffed), two choices for meat (pepperoni or ham), and four choices for toppings (mushrooms, pineapple, green peppers, extra cheese).

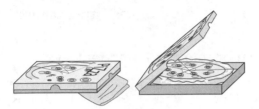

a) Draw a tree diagram to show how many different types of pizza she can order.

b) Verify the number of pizzas using multiplication.

c) If one of the guests is allergic to mushrooms, how many pizzas can Aira order? Use multiplication to verify your answer. Show your work.

5. Use a tree diagram and multiplication to find the outcomes of these three events.

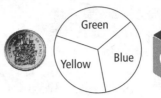

a) Tree diagram:

Multiplication:

b) How many possible outcomes are there?

6. a) Create a question that would give the following number of possible outcomes: $2 \times 5 \times 3 = 30$.

b) Draw a tree diagram to verify the number of possible outcomes.

11.3 Determining Probabilities Using Fractions

MathLinks 8, pages 426–435

Key Ideas Review

Choose from the terms below to complete #1.

experimental   multiplying   results   simulation   success   tables   tree diagrams

1. **a)** When you are finding probability using two or more independent events,

   you can find the probability by _____ the probabilities of

   _____ for each single event.

   b) There are three ways to find the probability of independent events:

   _____ , _____ , and _____ .

   c) A _____ is an experiment that can be used to model a real
   situation.

   d) The _____ of a simulation are called _____
   results.

Practise and Apply

2. Chad tosses this die and spins the
   spinner.

   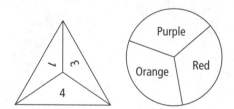

   a) Show the sample space.

   b) What is the probability of rolling
   a 4 and spinning purple?

   c) Verify your answer by multiplying
   each successful probability.

3. Jessie and Johan use their pencil
   cases to predict the probability of
   drawing the same pencil out of
   each case.

   a) What is the probability of them
   both choosing a grey pencil
   from their pencil cases? Use
   multiplication to find your answer.

   b) Verify your answer using a tree
   diagram.

4. The Grade 8 students have decided to decorate their school. Each class gets a part of the school to decorate. There are four Grade 8 classes: 8A, 8B, 8C, and 8D, and there are six available areas in the school: the foyer, library, hallway, gymnasium, cafeteria, and office. The students roll a six-sided die to determine which area they will decorate.

a) Design and describe a simulation to find the probability that 8C will get the foyer. Perform 20 trials. Record your results. What is the experimental probability of $P(8C, foyer)$?

5. Greg plays basketball for the school team. His statistics show he has a 60% chance of making his first foul shot and a 25% chance of making his second shot.

a) What is the probability of making both shots? Show your thinking.

b) Design and describe a simulation to find the experimental probability of him making both shots. Repeat the simulation 25 times. Record your results. What is $P(both shots)$?

b) Use multiplication to determine the theoretical probability of $P(8C, foyer)$. Show your answer as a fraction and a percent to two decimal places.

c) Compare your experimental and theoretical probability.

c) Compare the experimental probability and theoretical probability.

Link It Together

The annual street hockey tournament is next weekend. The Stribers do all the planning and they are ready with all the information. There are seven teams entered this year. Each team plays each of the other teams once as the home team. Note that they will also play each of the other teams as the visiting team once.

1. **a)** Draw a tree diagram to show the number of games that will be played and the teams that will play each other. Remember: You can't play your own team.

   b) How many games are played?

   c) Use multiplication to check your answer.

2. Josh Striber is on Team 3. He hopes his team can increase their number of wins this year compared to last year's two wins. He sets up a simulation to determine the probability.

   a) Create and describe a simulation to see if Josh could win more than two games this year. Explain any assumptions you make. Record the results of your simulation.

   b) What is the experimental probability for Josh's team winning more than two games?

Vocabulary Link

Draw a line from the example or description in column A to the correct term in column B, then find each term in the word search.

A	B
1. This is a successful result in a probability experiment.	a) experimental
2. This uses a model to find out what might happen in a real situation.	b) favourable outcome
3. In this type of event, the outcome of one event has no effect on the other. For example, you spin a spinner and then flip a coin.	c) independent
4. This includes all possible outcomes of a probability experiment.	d) probability
	e) sample space
5. Simulations are often used to develop this type of probability.	f) simulation
6. This refers to the likelihood of an event occurring.	g) theoretical
7. This is the calculated probability of an event occurring.	

```
H  X  F  Q  H  W  F  U  Z  J  E  I  Y  U  U  X  A  I  V  Z
N  F  D  R  X  X  A  B  D  J  X  K  E  J  Y  L  I  N  W  V
C  Y  Q  U  Z  V  V  V  J  J  P  R  N  L  N  W  L  D  W  T
M  M  E  P  Y  S  O  T  M  H  E  G  M  V  G  T  Q  E  F  W
M  F  D  O  F  A  U  R  R  X  R  A  V  Z  W  X  O  P  S  F
I  C  D  D  A  Z  R  Q  P  E  I  B  J  M  X  F  P  E  I  X
Z  W  G  B  Q  M  A  J  V  I  M  T  U  O  O  O  M  N  M  X
T  H  L  N  F  M  B  N  M  N  E  B  D  I  X  I  L  D  U  Z
K  Q  A  W  L  X  L  Y  D  Z  N  B  K  O  J  U  S  E  L  G
Q  Z  Q  O  T  H  E  O  R  E  T  I  C  A  L  Z  S  N  A  B
Z  D  M  S  Z  B  O  U  V  Z  A  H  O  L  W  E  J  T  T  L
G  B  N  P  P  L  U  M  A  H  L  T  D  N  I  B  E  N  I  K
N  S  W  C  J  Y  T  S  A  M  P  L  E  S  P  A  C  E  O  Q
T  H  C  F  D  E  C  C  Z  P  J  U  F  Z  J  J  C  C  N  K
A  M  W  Z  Z  I  O  S  P  R  O  B  A  B  I  L  I  T  Y  D
W  P  U  Q  J  R  M  U  F  Z  P  U  F  M  Q  T  J  C  T  S
F  M  X  A  C  P  E  X  N  I  N  B  C  V  V  Z  X  R  M  Z
R  V  H  L  A  D  B  I  N  Y  V  X  O  B  O  B  J  G  F  G
```

Congruent Figures

Congruent figures have the same shape and size. The equal sides and angles of congruent figures are called **corresponding** sides and angles. The △ABC is congruent to △DEF.

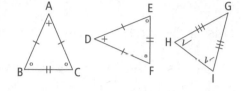

$$\angle A = \angle D$$

∠B and ∠C = ∠E and ∠F

$\overline{AB}$ and $\overline{AC}$ = $\overline{DE}$ and $\overline{DF}$

$$\overline{BC} = \overline{EF}$$

This could also be written as △ABC ≅ △DEF.

1. Are the figures in each pair congruent? Explain your reasoning.

a)
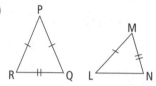

b)
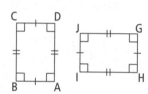

c)

d)

Characteristics of Regular Polygons

A **regular polygon** has all sides equal and all angles equal. An equilateral triangle is an example of a regular polygon. An **irregular polygon** is one that does not have all sides and angles equal. An isosceles triangle is an example of an irregular polygon.

regular polygon   irregular polygon

2. Decide if each polygon is regular or irregular. Give reasons for your decisions.

a)

b)

c)

d)

Transformations and Transformation Images

A **transformation** moves one geometric figure onto another.

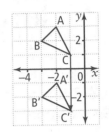

Transformations include translations, rotations, and reflections. The transformed figure is called an **image**.

• What translation is shown? What are the coordinates of the translation image?

△ABC has been translated 4 units vertically. The translation image is △A′B′C′. The coordinates are (−2, −1), (−3, −2), and (−1, −3).

• Rectangle PQRS has been reflected in the line of reflection, *m*. What are the coordinates of PQRS and its reflection image?

The coordinates of PQRS are (1, −2), (3, −2), (3, −1), and (1, −1). The coordinates of P′Q′R′S′ are (1, 4), (3, 4), (3, 3), and (1, 3).

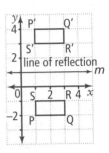

3. △THE is rotated around the centre of rotation, *z*.

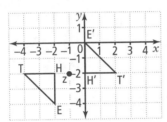

a) What are the coordinates of △THE and △T′H′E′?

b) What are the direction and angle of rotation?

4. Use the coordinate grid to complete the following questions.

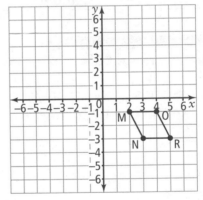

a) Translate parallelogram MORN 3 units up and 4 units left.

b) Draw a line of reflection, *t*, parallel to the *y*-axis at −2.

c) Reflect M′O′R′N′ in line of reflection *t*.

12.1 Exploring Tessellations With Regular and Irregular Polygons

MathLinks 8, pages 446–451

Key Ideas Review

Select words from column B to complete the statements in column A.

A	B
1. _____ are patterns that cover a plane without overlapping or gaps.	a) irregular
2. _____ types of _____ polygons can tessellate the plane.	b) regular
3. Some _____ polygons can tessellate the plane.	c) tessellations
4. Polygons tessellate the plane when interior angle measurements total 360° at the point where the _____ meet.	d) three e) vertices

Practise and Apply

5. Can you use these regular polygons to tessellate the plane? Justify your answer.

a)

b)

6. Draw a design in the space below by tessellating this shape.

7. Create two different designs using a rectangular brick. Here is one example:

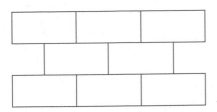

8. Find a tessellation either at home or at school and draw it below.

9. a) Describe how you know whether a shape can tessellate the plane.

b) Show two shapes by drawing examples, one that can tessellate the plane and one that cannot. Identify which one can tessellate the plane and which one cannot. Justify your response.

12.2 Constructing Tessellations Using Translations and Reflections

MathLinks 8, pages 452–456

Key Ideas Review

For #1 to #4, unscramble the letters to form a word that correctly completes the statement.

1. _____ can be made with two or more _____.
   LNSETSETLOIAS   GNYOLPSO

2. The _____ angles that meet must equal 360°.
          TROINERI

3. _____ and _____ are common
   OSLNAASTNIRT   RSNETFEOLIC
   transformations.

4. The area of a _____ is the same after it is
                        LTEI

   _____.
   MEDASRFONRT

Practise and Apply

5. What two polygons are used to form
   each tessellation?

   b)

   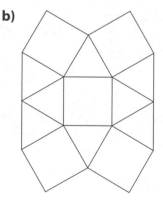

   a)

   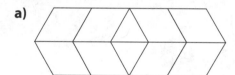

6. Use two or more polygons to create a tessellation.

8. What transformations are used to create each design below?

a)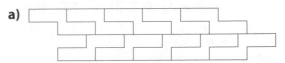

7. Levi wanted to redo his patio. He decided to use the letter "L" to tessellate a pattern.

L

a) Show a design that Levi might use.

b)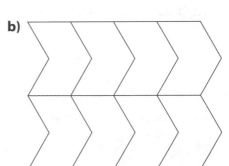

9. Create a design by using both translations and reflections.

b) Name at least four other letters that can tessellate the plane.

c) Draw a design using one of the letters you listed in b).

12.3 Constructing Tessellations Using Rotations

MathLinks 8, pages 457–460

Key Ideas Review

1. Decide whether each of the following statements is true or false. Circle the word *True* or *False*. If the statement is false, rewrite it to make it true.

   a) **True/False** Tessellations need more than two polygons to create a design.

   _____

   _____

   b) **True/False** Tessellations can be made if the interior angles of the polygons equal exactly 360° where the polygons meet.

   _____

   _____

   c) **True/False** Rotations cannot be used to create tessellations.

   _____

   _____

Practise and Apply

2. Name the polygons used in each design.

   a)

   b)

   c)

   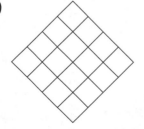

3. What transformations are used in each design in #2?

6. a) Choose two regular polygons that you can use to create a tessellation using rotations. Draw the design below.

4. Identify the shapes used in this design and their transformations.

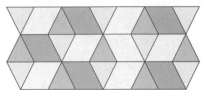

5. Choose a polygon that you can rotate to form a tessellation. Draw the design below.

b) Use those same two regular polygons to create a different design.

12.4 Constructing Escher-Style Tessellations

MathLinks 8, pages 461–465

Key Ideas Review

1. What steps should you take to create an Escher-style tessellation? Write the step number from column B that matches each description in column A.

A	B
a) Make sure there are no overlaps or gaps in the pattern. _____	Step 1
b) Use transformations to tessellate the plane. _____	Step 2
c) Use a regular or irregular polygon. _____	Step 3
d) Make sure the interior angles at vertices total exactly 360°. _____	Step 4
e) The area of the tessellating tile must remain unchanged. Any part of the tile that is cut out must be re-attached. _____	Step 5

Practise and Apply

2. State the transformations used in each design.

a)
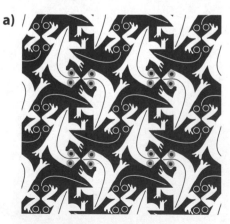

b)

3. Draw the original shape and explain or show how the tessellation could have been made.

a)

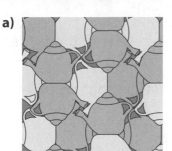

b)

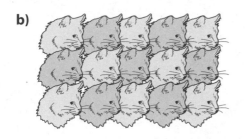

4. a) Create a tessellation using a square.

b) Use that square to create an Escher-style design below. Add details and colour to your design.

Link It Together

1. Your sister is having a birthday party this weekend and you are in charge of the craft area. She loves animals, so you decide to have your sister and her friends make an animal tessellation design.

   a) Use a square or equilateral triangle to create a tessellation that resembles an animal. Show the tile below.

   b) Make a list of the steps you will use to teach and carry out the activity at the party.

   Step 1 _____

   _____

   Step 2 _____

   _____

   Step 3 _____

   _____

   Step 4 _____

   _____

   Step 5 _____

   _____

   c) Use your tile from a) to make a sample to show your sister and her friends. Add details that will identify the animal.

Vocabulary Link

Unscramble the letters of each term. The terms are one to three words long. Use the clues to help you solve the puzzles.

A	B
1. This artist used tessellations to make unique pieces of art. _____	EHERCS
2. Here is a tile. This visual shows a _____ of the tile.	FSNTNRTOOIAMRA
3. This is a two-dimensional flat surface that extends in all directions. _____	PENLA
4. Here is a shape. In this visual, the shape is _____.	ITIEHNNTLGAPLE
5. This visual is not a _____ because the shapes overlap.	SELAENOTILST

Centimetre Grid Paper

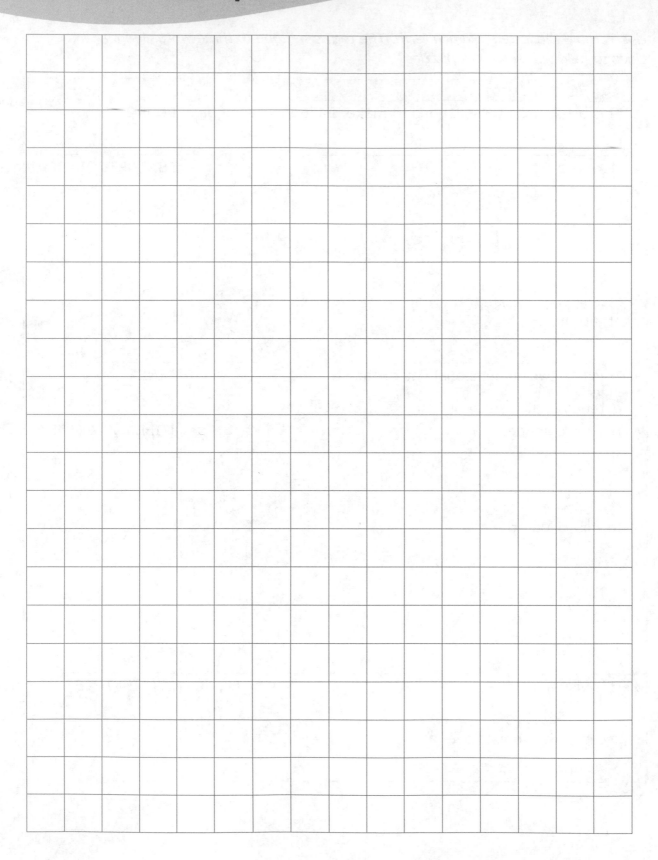

Centimetre Grid Paper

0.5 Centimetre Grid Paper

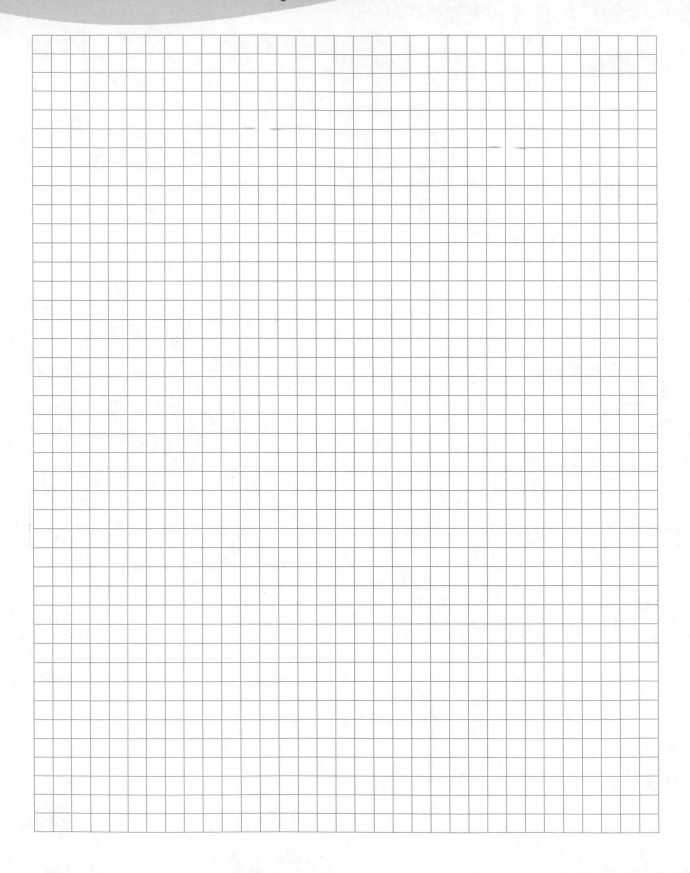

Name: _____   Date: _____

0.5 Centimetre Grid Paper

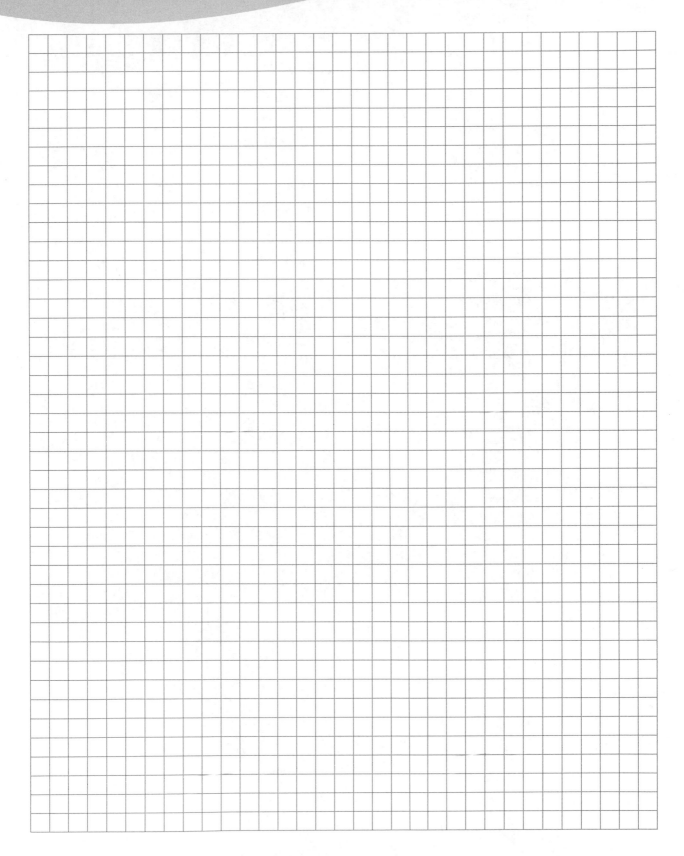

Isometric Dot Paper

Isometric Dot Paper

Workbook Answers

1 Get Ready

1. Answers may vary. Example: The location of the axes will change. The number of books will be along the *x*-axis; the type of books will be along the *y*-axis. The number of books for each bar will stay the same.

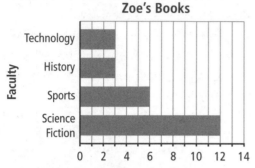

Zoe's Books

2. **a)** 10
   b) Answers may vary. Example: Who has the most books in total? They have the same number of books.

3. **a)** Chat Lines, 10 h
   b) No. Answers will vary. Example: Because there is no legend, the reader would not know what each sector of the graph represents.

4. **a)** Between April and May
   b) Answers may vary. Example: Yes, the trend will continue because of the seasons.

5. **a)** 40
   b) Answers may vary. Example: I added the total of full T-shirts and multiplied that by 10. Then, I added the half shirts and multiplied that by 5. I then added the two figures together.

1.1 Advantages and Disadvantages of Different Graphs

1. **d)** Circle graphs
2. **b)** Line graphs
3. **e)** Double bar graphs

4. **c)** Pictographs
5. **a)** Bar graphs
6. **a)** 30 more Grade 9s attended the dance. Answers may vary. Example: This is shown easily on the pictograph by multiplying the number of symbols times 12.
   b) Answers may vary. Example: You can easily calculate the number using the pictograph. Using the circle graph, you would have to calculate 12% of 300.
   c) Answers may vary. Example: Circle graph: You can see at a glance the largest group that attended. Pictograph: This graph lets you calculate actual numbers easily.

7. **a)** 16 more in November than September. Answers may vary. Example: The pictograph showed this clearly. The line graph has a large scale, so the exact number for each month is not clear—you would have to estimate.
   b) Between October and November.
   c) Answers may vary. Example: Line graph: The exact amounts are not clear, based on the scale used. Pictograph: You have to multiply to determine the number for each month.

8. Answers may vary. Example:
   a)

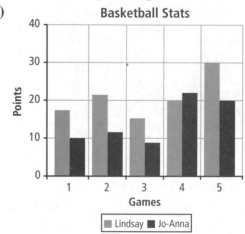

Basketball Stats

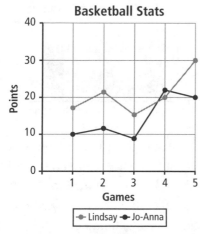

Basketball Stats

Legend: Lindsay, Jo-Anna

b) Answers may vary. Example: They both show the data given. To compare growth over time, the line graph is better. To look at the total number of points, the bar graph is better.

9. Answers may vary. Example:

a) I would draw a bar graph to show the comparison of each type of game. This would easily display the most popular and least popular type of game.

b) No, a line graph is best used for showing change over time. These data show the amount sold; they do not include any length of time.

1.2 Misrepresenting Data

1. a) data, false **b)** scale, visuals

2. a) Answers may vary. Example: Because of the break in the y-axis, this graph leads you to believe that Tina sold significantly more than Tim or Ty. The title also suggests that.

b) $500

c) Answers may vary. Example: The graph should be drawn using a proper scale and the title should be Employee Sales.

3. Answers may vary. Example:

a) Graph A shows rainfall by centimetres and Graph B by millimetres, but the amounts work out to be the same.

b) Because Graph A uses values in 10s and the bars look shorter, people might think Graph A shows less precipitation than Graph B shows.

c) I think the director should choose Graph A, because it looks like there is less rainfall when the amounts are shown in centimetres.

4. a) Tigers, by 6%

Answers may vary. Example:

b) The larger graphic and the title suggest that the difference in the number of fans supporting each team was significantly greater than it actually was.

c) You could draw a circle graph to show the difference in attendance.

5. a) 2 km

b) Answers may vary. Example: I would redraw the graph using bars the same width, and change the scale to show the difference more accurately.

6. Answers will vary. Example:

Keisha's Practice Time

I used a bar graph with a large interval on the vertical axis to make the bars seem really large. I reversed the weeks on the horizontal axis to make it appear as though the band is practising longer each week.

1.3 Critiquing Data Presentation

1. c) usefulness

2. b) format

3. a) type

4. Answers may vary. Example:

a) It shows the comparison of all the snacks and makes it easier to see which are the most popular.

b) This graph does not show the other snacks that may be in the vending machine already, so there is no comparison and we do not know why the snacks should be changed.

5. Answers may vary. Example:

a) The conclusions are that one park has three activities and the other has one.

b) No, this is not the best graph, maybe use separate bar graphs showing all the types of activities in each park.

6. Answers may vary. Example:

a) The bar graph shows the number of positions available for each job each month, and the circle graph shows the percent of students working in each type of job.

b) The bar graph shows more information about job availability throughout the months; there is more of a chance to get a job in June or July with baseball, but delivering flyers remains steady.

c) The circle graph shows that about the same percent of students work at each job.

7. Answers may vary. Example:

a) This graph shows that Stephanie had five main interests that week: sports, computer, visiting, shopping, and reading. It also shows how she divided her spare time that week.

b) This graph shows that Stephanie has several interests. She appears to share her time among her five main interests, with a little more time spent playing sports. There is no indication of how long Stephanie spends doing each activity.

① Link It Together

1. Answers may vary. Example:

a) I believe the best way to show the data would be a bar graph because a bar graph will clearly compare the student preferences across flavours.

b)

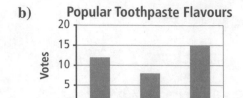

Popular Toothpaste Flavours

c) One advantage of a bar graph is that you can clearly see the comparison between all three flavours, which one has the most votes, and which one the least votes. One disadvantage is that, depending on the scale, the exact number of votes could be difficult to identify.

2. a) Answers may vary. Example: You can mislead the reader by making the peppermint bar wider, which may make it appear more popular.

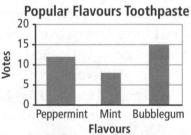

Popular Flavours Toothpaste

b) You could use a circle graph or a pictograph to show the same information. A circle graph would show the fraction of votes each flavour received. A pictograph would show the number of votes each flavour received.

① Vocabulary Link

1. double bar graph
2. bar graph
3. trend
4. line graph
5. distort
6. circle graph
7. pictograph
8. interval
9. double line graph

2 Get Ready

1. a) 3 to 6, 3:6, $\frac{3}{6}$ b) 6 to 9, 6:9, $\frac{6}{9}$

2. a) white balls : black balls
   b) black balls : total balls

3. a) Yes, because $2 \times 3 = 6$, and $3 \times 3 = 9$.
   b) Yes, because $1 \times 4 = 4$, and $5 \times 4 = 20$.

4. Answers may vary.
   a) $\frac{2}{8}, \frac{3}{12}$ b) $\frac{2}{6}, \frac{8}{24}$

5. a) 15, because $8 \times 3 = 24$, and $5 \times 3 = 15$.
   b) 15, because $1 \times 5 = 5$, and $3 \times 5 = 15$.
   Comparing Quantities: Answers may vary.
   For example: I would reuse the $\frac{2}{5}$ number
   line and number by tens.

6. Answers may vary. $\frac{14}{28}, \frac{2}{4}, \frac{7}{14}$

7. a) 10 b) 3

2.1 Two-Term and Three-Term Ratios

1. a) **False** A part-to-part ratio compares
   different parts of a group.
   b) **True**
   c) **False** A part-to-whole ratio can be
   written as a fraction, decimal, or percent.
   For example, the ratio of flowers to leaves
   is $\frac{8}{12}$ or $\frac{2}{3}$, $0.6\overline{6}$, $66.\overline{6}\%$
   d) **True**
   e) **False** A two-term ratio compares two
   quantities measured in the same units.

2. a) 3:9, 1:3   b) 23:9:32
   c) 5:15, 1:3 d) 8:6, 4:3
   e) 10:20;1:2 f) 16:20, 4:5

3. a) $\frac{1}{3} = \frac{2}{6}$ b) $\frac{2}{3} = \frac{10}{15}$ c) $\frac{5}{6} = \frac{10}{12}$ d) $\frac{40}{50} = \frac{80}{100}$

4. Answers may vary. Example:
   a)
   b) 9:3
   c) 9:12, 3:12
   d) $\frac{3}{4}, \frac{1}{4}$

5. Answers may vary. Example:
   a) hats : coats
   b) coats : hooks : hats
   c) hooks : coats
   d) hooks : whole

6. a) 8:28
   b) 20:8

7. 0.18:0.35:0.47

2.2 Rates

1. a) different b) fraction, percent
   c) one   d) price

2. a) 16.67 km/h   b) 66 words/minute
   c) 54 students/bus d) 23 apples/bag
   e) $9/h   f) 88 km/h

3. a) $7/h, $\boxed{\$9.90/h}$ b) 82 km/h, $\boxed{84\text{ km/h}}$
   c) $\boxed{4\text{ h/day}}$, 3 h/day

4. 9 L/100 km

5. a) Vanilla $0.00745/g, Berry $0.00598/g,
      Peach $0.0049875/g
   b) Vanilla $0.745 /100 g, Berry $0.598/100 g,
      $\boxed{\text{Peach }\$0.49875/100\text{ g}}$
   c) The largest (peach) container costs the least
      money per gram.

6. a) Methods will vary. Example:
      $\frac{1365}{6} = \frac{x}{12}$, $x = \$2730$
   b) $5.25/h

7. a) Canada 3.36, Ecuador 45.19, France
      108.02, Netherlands 464.94, USA 29.77
   b) Netherlands, France, Ecuador, USA,
      Canada
   c) Yes, because it compares two quantities
      measured in different units.

2.3 Proportional Reasoning

1. ratios, equal

2. a) proportion, $15 b) unit rate, $15

3. a) 25 km/h b) $0.25/pencil
   c) 5 m/s   d) $2/kg

4. a) 3 b) 3 c) 25 d) 12

5. a) 8 roses b) 760 km

6. a) $\frac{40\text{ cm}}{20\text{ cm}} = \frac{50\text{ cm}}{25\text{ cm}}$
   b) $\frac{60\text{ mL}}{600\text{ mL}} = \frac{100\text{ mL}}{1000\text{ mL}}$
   c) $\frac{9.4\text{ L}}{100\text{ km}} = \frac{56.4\text{ L}}{600\text{ km}}$

7. 24 players

8. a) $\frac{5}{8} = \frac{x}{40}$ Trevor is expected to complete 25 passes.

   b) $\frac{1}{16} = \frac{x}{32}$ He likely made 2 interceptions.

9. a) 16, 24 **b)** $1.38, $9.66

10. Car A   **11.** 150 km

② Link It Together

1. a) 2 : 3

b)

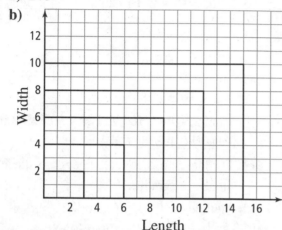

Rect-angle	Length	Width	Area (square units)	Area Difference (square units)
P	3	2	6	-
Q	6	4	24	18
R	9	6	54	30
S	12	8	96	42
T	15	10	150	54

d) $\frac{2}{3}$ **e)** 216 square units

② Vocabulary Link

1. c) proportion
2. h) unit rate
3. g) unit price
4. a) part-to-part ratio
5. b) part-to-whole ratio
6. f) two-term ratio

7. e) three-term ratio
8. d) rate

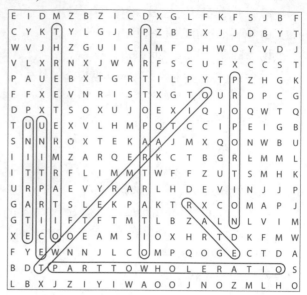

③ Get Ready

1. a) Answers may vary. Example:

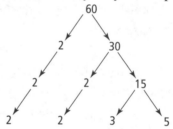

   b) 1 and 60, 2 and 30, 3 and 20, 4 and 15, 5 and 12, 6 and 10

2. 1 and 12, 2 and 6, 3 and 4

3. a) 56 cm   **b)** 33 m²

4. a) 5, 6, 7, 8

   b) 26, 27, 28, 29, 30, 31, 32, 33, 34, 35

5. a) 6.5 **b)** 30.5

6. a) 7 **b)** 16

7. a) 6 **b)** 3

③.1 Squares and Square Roots

1. d) Prime number
2. b) Square number

3. e) Square root
4. c) Perfect square
5. a) Prime factorization
6. a) $2 \times 2 \times 3 \times 3$
    b) Yes. Answers may vary. Example: There is one pair of 2s and one pair of 3s. $2 \times 3 = 6, 6 \times 6 = 36$
    c) Answers may vary. Example:

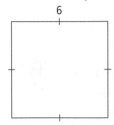

6

7. a) $2 \times 2 \times 5 \times 5$
    b) Yes. Answers may vary. Example: There is one pair of 2s and one pair of 5s. $2 \times 5 = 10, 10 \times 10 = 100$
    c) Answers may vary. Example:

10 m

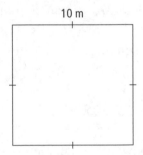

8. a) $2 \times 2 \times 41$
    b) $2 \times 2 \times 7 \times 7$, perfect square
    c) $3 \times 3 \times 5 \times 5$, perfect square
    d) $13 \times 5 \times 5$

9. Strategies may vary. Example: $1296 = 2 \times 2 \times 2 \times 2 \times 3 \times 3 \times 3 \times 3$. 1296 is a perfect square because it is the product of 36×36.

10. Yes. Answers may vary. Example: The prime factors of 9 and 16 repeat themselves. 9 is the product of 3×3 and 16 is the product of $2 \times 2 \times 2 \times 2$. The prime factors repeat themsclves an even number of times. 10 is not a perfect square because its prime factors do not repeat themselves.

3.2 Exploring the Pythagorean Relationship

1. a) Answers may vary. Two are possible:
    - Area of R + Area of S = Area of T
    - $d^2 + e^2 = f^2$
    b) Answers may vary. Example: The sum of the areas of the squares attached to the legs of a right triangle is equal to the area of the square attached to the hypotenuse.

2. a) $J = 36 \text{ m}^2, K = 64 \text{ m}^2, L = 100 \text{ m}^2$
    b) Answers may vary and should include two of the following:
    - $36 \text{ m}^2 + 64 \text{ m}^2 = 100 \text{ m}^2$
    - $6^2 + 8^2 = 10^2$
    - Area of J + Area of K = Area of L

3. a) 64 cm^2, 8 cm; 225 cm^2, 15 cm; 289 cm^2, 17 cm
    b) Answers may vary and should include one of the following:
    - $64 \text{ cm}^2 + 225 \text{ cm}^2 = 289 \text{ cm}^2$
    - $8^2 + 15^2 = 17^2$

4. a) $225 \text{ cm}^2, 400 \text{ cm}^2, 625 \text{ cm}^2$
    b) Answers may vary and should include one of the following:
    - $225 \text{ m}^2 + 400 \text{ m}^2 = 625 \text{ m}^2$
    - $15^2 + 20^2 = 25^2$

5. Yes. Answers may vary. Example: The area of the square on the hypotenuse equals the total of the areas of the squares on each of the two legs.

6. a) 61 cm^2 b) 51 cm^2
7. a) 130 cm^2 b) 241 mm^2
8. Yes. Answers may vary. Example: The areas of the squares on the two smaller sides are 9 m^2 and 16 m^2. These add up to 25 m^2, which is the area of the square on the longest side.

3.3 Estimating Square Roots

1. Answers may vary for estimates. Example:
    a) 6.3   b) 14
2. a) whole, exact
    b) decimal, approximation

3. **a)** 4, 9 **b)** 16, 25 **c)** 64, 81 **d)** 81, 100
4. 26, 27, 28, 29, 30, 31, 32, 33, 34, 35
5. Answers may vary for estimates. Example:
   a) 4.1 **b)** 9.2
6. Answers may vary for estimates.
   a) 25, 36, 5.2 **b)** 49, 64, 7.4
   c) 100, 121, 10.2 **d)** 121, 144, 11.8
7. Answers may vary for estimates. Example:
   6.7 cm
8. 15
9. **a)** Answers may vary for estimates.
   Example: 7.7 m
   b) Yes. Answers may vary. Example: If each
   side is about 7.7 m, multiply that times 4
   to get 30.8 m, which is less than 32 m.
10. Answers may vary. Example: The
    maximum size of the rug should be
    approximately 14.4 m².

3.4 Using the Pythagorean Relationship

1. Pythagorean, length, hypotenuse, legs
2. **a)** 10 m **b)** 36 cm
3. **a)** 41 cm **b)** 37 m
4. **a)** 12 cm **b)** 12 cm
5. **a)** 3.3 cm **b)** 9.7 cm
6. 10.2 cm
7. **a)** 4.5 m **b)** 17 m
8. No. Answers may vary. Example: The areas
   of the squares on each leg add to 13 m². The
   area of the square on the long side is 25 m².
   If the ramp had a right triangle, these two
   values would be equal.

3.5 Applying the Pythagorean Relationship

1. **a)** Answers are in italics.
   $d^2 = 12^2 + 5^2$
   $d^2 = 144 + 25$
   $d^2 = 169$
   $d = \sqrt{169}$
   $d = 13$
   The hypotenuse is 13 km long.

b) Answers are in italics.
   $15^2 + 20^2 = 25^2$
   Left side: $15^2 + 20^2 = 225 + 400$
   $\qquad\qquad\qquad\qquad = 625$
   Right side: $25^2 = 625$
   Yes, Yes
2. 12.7 cm
3. 100 m
4. 5.9 m
5. 6.9 cm
6. **a)** 15 cm **b)** 120 cm²
7. No. Answers may vary. Example: The
   corners do not meet at right angles
   because $17^2 + 26^2 \neq 31^2$.
8. 250 km

3 Link It Together

1. Answers are in italics.
   a) Factors: 1, 2, *4*, 8, 16; square root: *4*
   b) Factors: 1, 3, *9*, 27, 81; square root: *9*
   c) Factors: 1, *2*, *3*, 4, *6*, *8*, *12*, 18, 24, *36*,
      48, 72, 144; square root: *12*
   d) Factors: 1, *5*, 15, 45, *225*;
      square root: *15*
   e) Factors: *1*, 5, *25*, *125*, 625;
      square root: *25*
2. **a)** Drawings may vary. Example:

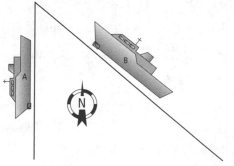

b) Rescue boat A: $\frac{36}{60} = \frac{3}{5}$, $\frac{3}{5}$h $\times$ 15 km/h =
   9 km.
   Rescue boat B: $\frac{45}{60} = \frac{3}{4}$, $\frac{3}{4} \times$ 20 km/h =
   15 km.
c) $x^2 = 15^2 - 9^2$, $x^2 = 225 - 81$, $x^2 = 144$,
   $x = \sqrt{144}$, $x = 12$. The rescue boats
   were 12 km apart when they started.

3 Vocabulary Link

Across

2. perfect square
4. Pythagorean relationship

Down

1. square root
2. prime factorization
3. hypotenuse
5. legs

4 Get Ready

1. a) 25% b) 89% c) 64%

2. a)
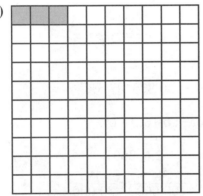

b)
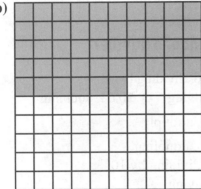

c)
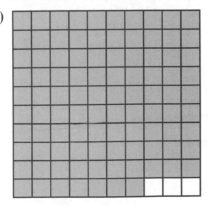

3. a) $\frac{1}{4}$ or 0.25 or 25%

 b) $\frac{3}{8}$ or 0.375 or 37.5%

 c) $\frac{1}{2}$ or 0.50 or 50%

 d) $\frac{4}{5}$ or 0.80 or 80%

4. a) $0.\overline{3}$ b) $0.\overline{45}$ c) $0.\overline{27}$

5. a) $0.\overline{81}$ or $81.\overline{81}$%   b) $0.\overline{7}$ or $77.\overline{7}$%
 c) $0.8\overline{3}$ or $83.\overline{3}$%

6. Estimates may vary.
 a) 17 b) 51 c) 52 d) 72

4.1 Representing Percents

1. c) shade more than one grid

2. a) shade squares from a hundred grid to show the whole number and part of one square to show the fraction

3. d) shade squares on a grid of 100 squares called a hundred grid

4. b) shade part of one square on a hundred grid

5. a) 144%   b) $\frac{2}{3}$% c) 88.8%

6. a) $135\frac{7}{8}$% b) 256% c) $\frac{7}{12}$%

7. a)
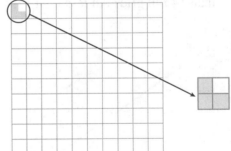

b)
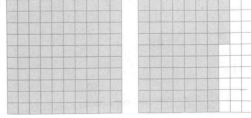

8. a)

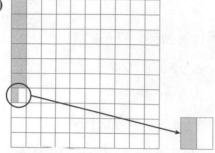

b)

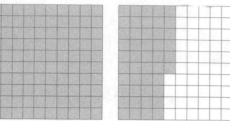

9. a) 3. Explanations will vary. Example: You need 3 full grids because 230% is more than 2 full grids but less than 3.

b) 7. Explanations will vary. Example: You need 7 full grids because 680% is more than 7 full grids but less than 8.

c) 4. Explanations will vary. Example: You need 4 full grids because 395% is more than 3 full grids but less than 4.

d) 15. Explanations will vary. Example: You need 15 full grids because 1420% is more than 14 full grids but less than 15.

10.

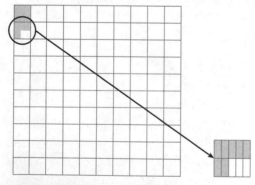

11.

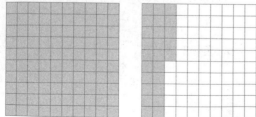

1. hundred grid, division, 0.15, 0.15

2. hundred grids, multiplication, 226%, 226%

3. fractions, decimals

4. **a)** 0.75 or 75% **b)** 0.07 or 7%
   c) 1.8 or 180% **d)** 0.125 or 12.5%
   e) 0.0375 or 3.75%

5. **a)** 425% or $\frac{425}{100} = 17/4$

   b) 84.5% or $\frac{845}{1000} = \frac{169}{200}$

   c) 0.62% or $\frac{62}{10\ 000} = \frac{31}{5000}$

6. **a)** 7.35 or $\frac{735}{100} = \frac{147}{20}$

   b) 0.165 or $\frac{165}{1000} = \frac{33}{200}$

   c) 0.006 or $\frac{6}{1000} = \frac{3}{500}$

7. 125%

8. **a)** $\frac{21}{24}$ or $\frac{7}{8}$, 0.875, 87.5%

   b) $\frac{5}{30}$ or $\frac{1}{6}$, $0.1\overline{6}$, $16.\overline{6}$%

   c) $\frac{65}{25}$ or $\frac{13}{5}$, 2.6, 260%

9. 0.00038, $\frac{38}{100\ 000}$ or $\frac{19}{50\ 000}$

10. 26.9%

4.3 **Percent of a Number**

1. **a)** $0.66, dividing by ten
   b) 9, halving **c)** $0.64, doubling

2. decimal, multiply

3. **a)** 9000, doubling
   b) 0.6, dividing by 10
   c) 1, halving
   d) 21, dividing by 10
   e) 12, doubling, dividing by 10
   f) 1350, doubling, halving

4. **a)** 1.26 **b)** 71.63 **c)** $874.16
   d) 501.88 **e)** $467.82

5. $23 287.50

6. 3094 mg

7. Estimates may vary.
    a) $1000, $916.50
    b) 1 600 000, 1 792 000   **c)** 3000, 3087

8. 6621 km

4.4 Combining Percents

1. d)

2. a)

3. c)

4. b)

5. Estimates may differ.
    a) $134, $134.47   **b)** $ 24.20, $23.73
    c) $36.80, $35.03   **d)** $38.40, $38.47

6. 46

7. **a)** $67.20

    b) Yes. Explanations will vary. Example: a
    50% off sale would have resulted in a
    $60 price. This did not happen with the
    first sale because the second price change
    gave 20% off the first sale price. This was
    less than 20% off the original price.

8. **a)** $180 **b)** $199.80

9. 0.93 km²

10. $438.15

11. 22

12. $9.68/h

4 Link It Together

1. **a)**

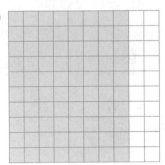

192 students

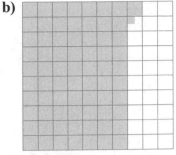

171 students

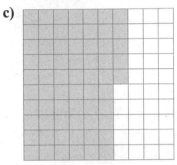

c)

312 attendees

2. **a)** Grids will vary. Example:

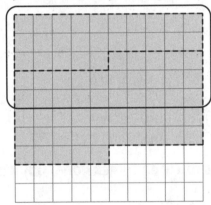

50%

    b) 420

    c) Answers will vary. Example: $66\frac{2}{3}$% of
    the students who attended brought two
    adults. This is a percent of the percent of
    students who attended. So, it is a smaller
    percent than $66\frac{2}{3}$% of the entire school
    population.

4 Vocabulary Link

1. d) greater than one

2. f) one

3. g) percent

4. c) fractional percent

5. b) double

6. e) halve

7. a) combined percent

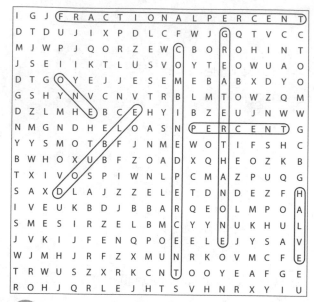

5 Get Ready

1. a) rectangular prism; 6; 12; 8

   b) trangular prism; 5; 9; 6

   c) cube; 6; 12; 8

2. a) 22.0 cm   b) 12.6 cm²

3. a) 16.5 cm²   b) 50 cm²   c) 30 cm²

5.1 Views of Three-Dimensional Objects

1. a) three, 3-D

   b) top, front, side, draw, build, 3-D

2. top, side, front

3.

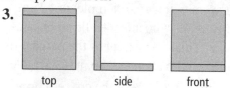

top   side   front

4. a)

   b)

5. top   front   side

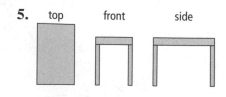

6. a)

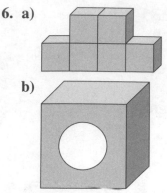

   b)

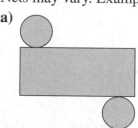

7. top: A; front: C; side: E

5.2 Nets of Three-Dimensional Objects

1. a) net   b) 3-D object

2. Nets may vary. Example:

   a)

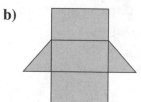

   b)

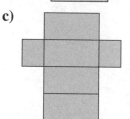

   c)

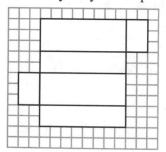

3. Nets may vary. Example:

4. Make sure all results fold into a cube.
   Answers will vary; here are examples:

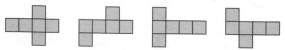

5. Answers will vary; here is an example:

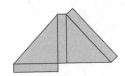

6. a)

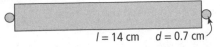

$l = 14$ cm $d = 0.7$ cm

b) Nets may vary. Example: This box will have extra room around the pencils.

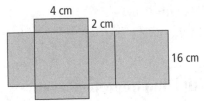

4 cm
2 cm
16 cm

5.3 Surface Area of a Prism

1. face, surface area
2. **a)** 220.6 cm² **b)** 451.2 cm²
3. **a)** 120 m² **b)** 140.1 m²
4. 3.13 m²
5. 124.5 m²
6. **a)** 7.74 m² **b)** $193.11

5.4 Surface Area of a Cylinder

1. **a)** add, area **b)** cylinder **c)** circumference
2. Nets may vary. Example:

3. **a)** 1800 cm² **b)** 54 mm²
4. 52.99 cm²
5. **a)** 505.54 mm² **b)** 469.82 km²
6. **a)** 229.8 cm²
   b) Answers may vary. The following is based on a container of 5.5 cm high and 13 cm in diameter (to give a little extra room in the container): 489.84 cm²

5 Link It Together

1.

Top
Front
Side
Tunnel

Top
Front
Side
Pause Table

2. Nets may vary. The net for the tunnel should not show any ends. Example:

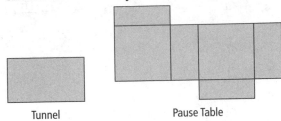

Tunnel

Pause Table

3. Tunnel = 10.36 m², Pause Table = 3.64 m²

5 Vocabulary Link

Across

4. rectangular prism
6. triangular prism

Down

1. surface area
2. cylinder
3. prisms
5. net

6 Get Ready

1. **a)** $\frac{1}{3}$ **b)** $\frac{5}{6}$ **c)** $\frac{7}{10}$
2. **a)** $\frac{1}{4}$ **b)** $\frac{1}{2}$ **c)** $\frac{2}{15}$
3. **a)** $3\frac{4}{5}$ **b)** 6 **c)** $1\frac{1}{5}$ **d)** $5\frac{3}{7}$
4. **a)** $4\frac{3}{8}$ **b)** $7\frac{3}{10}$
5. **a)** $2\frac{1}{6}$ **b)** $2\frac{1}{4}$
6. **a)** 1 **b)** 4

6.1 Multiplying a Fraction and a Whole Number

1. multiplication **a)** 3, 3 **b)** 2, 2
   c) 3, 12, 3
2. fraction, either, $\frac{2}{3}$
3. **a)** $4 \times \frac{1}{6} = \frac{2}{3}$ **b)** $3 \times \frac{1}{2} = 1\frac{1}{2}$
   c) $4 \times \frac{1}{3} = 1\frac{1}{3}$
4. **a)** $4 \times \frac{2}{3} = \frac{8}{3}$ or $2\frac{2}{3}$ **b)** $2 \times \frac{8}{5} = \frac{16}{5}$ or $3\frac{1}{5}$
   c) $6 \times \frac{1}{7} = \frac{6}{7}$
5. **a)** $1\frac{1}{5}$ **b)** $2\frac{1}{2}$
6. **a)** 2 **b)** $\frac{8}{9}$
7. **a)** $\frac{3}{4}$ **b)** $\frac{5}{8}$ **c)** 2 **d)** 5 **e)** $1\frac{1}{2}$
8. 6 h
9. $2\frac{3}{4}$
10. Methods will vary. 225 m

6.2 Dividing a Fraction by a Whole Number

1. b)
2. c)
3. a)
4. **a)** $\frac{1}{6}$ **b)** $\frac{5}{12}$
5. **a)** $\frac{1}{12}$ **b)** $\frac{5}{18}$
6. **a)** $\frac{2}{9}$ **b)** $\frac{3}{10}$
7. **a)** $\frac{2}{3} \div 4$ **b)** Diagrams will vary. $\frac{1}{6}$
8. **a)** $\frac{3}{5}$ m $\div 2$ **b)** Diagrams will vary. $\frac{3}{10}$ m
9. **a)** Expressions may vary. Example:
   $\frac{9}{12} \div 4 = \frac{9}{48}$ or $\frac{3}{16}$
   b) Diagrams will vary.

6.3 Multiplying Proper Fractions

1. paper folding
2. numerators, multiply
3. estimate

4. **a)** $1, \frac{5}{9}$ **b)** $0, \frac{4}{45}$ **c)** $\frac{1}{4}, \frac{3}{20}$
   d) $\frac{1}{2}, \frac{6}{15}$ or $\frac{2}{5}$ **e)** $\frac{1}{2}, \frac{21}{40}$ **f)** $1, \frac{4}{5}$
5. $\frac{1}{4}$ km
6. $\frac{1}{8}$
7. $\frac{1}{2}, \frac{1}{2}$
8. Québec's population is approximately $\frac{2}{15}$ the population of Toronto.
9. Models will vary. $\frac{1}{25}$
10. $\frac{1}{12}$

6.4 Multiplying Improper Fractions and Mixed Numbers

1. **a)** **True**
   b) **False** You can estimate the product of two mixed numbers or improper fractions by multiplying the whole numbers closest to them.
   c) **False** Two mixed numbers can be multiplied by expressing them as improper fractions and then multiplying the numerators and multiplying the denominators.
2. **a)** $1\frac{4}{5}$ **b)** $2\frac{1}{6}$
3. **a)** $\frac{5}{2}$ **b)** $\frac{14}{3}$
4. Models will vary.
   a) $\frac{1}{2}$ **b)** 3
5. **a)** $1, \frac{4}{5}$ **b)** $8, 9\frac{1}{3}$ **c)** $6, 5\frac{5}{6}$
6. **a)** $10\frac{1}{2}$ h **b)** $94.50
7. $16\frac{4}{5}$
8. $11\frac{1}{3}$ km
9. $2\frac{4}{5}$ h
10. 3 tanks
11. 18 years old
12. $9\frac{3}{4}$ h

6.5 Dividing Fractions and Mixed Numbers

1. b)

2. c)

3. a)

4. d)

5. a) $2\frac{1}{2}$ b) 2 c) $\frac{2}{3}$ d) $2\frac{5}{8}$

6. a) $\frac{4}{5}$ b) $2\frac{1}{2}$ c) $1\frac{3}{8}$ d) $\frac{15}{23}$

7. a) $\frac{15}{16}$ b) $1\frac{1}{2}$ c) $3\frac{1}{7}$ d) $2\frac{2}{3}$

8. a) $2, 1\frac{1}{2}$ b) $1\frac{1}{2}, 1\frac{6}{13}$

   c) $2, 1\frac{9}{17}$

9. a) $1\frac{3}{4}, 1\frac{20}{21}$ b) $2\frac{2}{3}, 3\frac{1}{33}$

   c) $1\frac{3}{4}, 1\frac{25}{32}$

10. 18

11. 5

12. $3\frac{3}{5}$ km/h

13. $3\frac{3}{4}$

6.6 Applying Fraction Operations

1. a) operation b) order

2. 3, 1, 2

3. a) $\frac{1}{3} \times \frac{3}{4}, \frac{7}{12}$ b) $\left(1\frac{1}{2} + \frac{5}{6}\right), 2\frac{1}{3}$

   c) $\frac{7}{8} + \frac{2}{3}, \frac{7}{24}$ d) $1\frac{1}{2} \times \frac{1}{3}, \frac{3}{4}$

4. a) $6\frac{1}{2}$ b) $\frac{17}{18}$ c) $2\frac{5}{8}$ d) $1\frac{5}{32}$

5. $528

6. $\left(1\frac{1}{2} \times \frac{1}{4}\right) \div 3 = \frac{5}{12}$

7. a) $\left(\frac{1}{2} + \frac{5}{8}\right) \times \frac{4}{3} + \frac{3}{2} = 3$

   b) $1\frac{1}{4} - \frac{1}{8} \div \left(1\frac{1}{2} - \frac{3}{4}\right) = 1\frac{1}{12}$

   c) $\frac{13}{5} - \left(\frac{3}{10} + \frac{7}{10}\right) \div \frac{1}{2} - \frac{3}{5} = 0$

   d) $1\frac{1}{4} \times \left(2\frac{2}{5} \div 2\frac{1}{6}\right) - 1\frac{1}{3} = \frac{2}{39}$

8. Answers may vary. Examples:

   a) $\frac{3}{3} \times 3 - 3$

   b) $3 + \frac{3}{3} - 3$

   c) $\frac{3}{3} + \frac{3}{3}$

   d) $3 + (3 - 3) \times 3$

9. Expressions may vary. Example:

   $2000 \times \left(\frac{1}{2} + \frac{1}{5}\right) = 1400$, 1400 km

6 Link It Together

1. a) 16 L b) $15\frac{11}{12}$ L

2. $41.25

3. 5 L

4. $31.25

6 Vocabulary Link

1. denominator
2. reciprocal
3. commutative property
4. numerator
5. proper fraction
6. quotient
7. product
8. order of operations
9. mixed number
10. dividend
11. improper fraction
12. divisor

7 Get Ready

1. The right prisms are a) and c) and the right cylinder is f). These figures have faces that meet the base at 90°.

2. Answers will vary.
   a) between 175 and 200
   b) between 720 and 800
   c) between 140 and 210

3. a) 416 cm² b) 123.8 m² c) 226.5 cm²

4. a) $4 \times 4 \times 4 = 64$
   b) $3 \times 3 \times 3 \times 3 \times 3 = 243$

5. No, 3 to the power of 4 is $3 \times 3 \times 3 \times 3$, which is 81, and 4 to the power of 3 is $4 \times 4 \times 4$, which is 64.

7.1 Understanding Volume

1. a) cylinder/prism, prism/cylinder, base, height
   b) does not

2. a)

   b)

3. a) 756 cm³ b) 162 cm³
4. a) 400 cm³ b) 339 cm³ c) 960 cm³
5. 105 cm³
6. a) Both have a volume of 200 cm³.
   b) Both have a volume of 10.5 m³.
7. a) 7 cm b) 6.5 m
8. 24.3 m³
9. The chocolate bar on the left has less chocolate.

7.2 Volume of a Prism

1. b
2. c
3. a
4. a) 540 cm³ b) 119 m³ c) 2560 cm³
5. a) 91.1 cm³ b) 343 cm³
6. a) 162 cm³ b) 63.8 m³ c) 120 m³
7. a) 384 cm³ b) 672 m³ c) 39 cm³
8. The taller container on the left contains more juice.
9. 7.2 m³

7.3 Volume of a Cylinder

1. circle
2. area, circle
3. volume, cylinder, area
4. a) 2119.5 cm³ b) 2034.72 cm³ c) 0.15 m³
5. a) 1538.6 cm³ b) 14.47 m³
6. a) 1695.6 cm³ b) 3229.49 cm³
   c) 113.04 m³ d) 5000.45 cm³
7. a) 471 cm³ b) 8 cm
8. 0.064 m³

7.4 Solving Problems Involving Prisms and Cylinders

1. a) prisms, cylinders b) formula c) diagram
2. calculations
3. a) Diagrams will vary. b) 22
4. a) 788.53 cm³ b) 938.47 cm³
5. Cheyenne
6. a) Answers will vary. Example: I will fit five bead containers across the bottom row, then I will put four bead containers upside down on top of these five containers. I will build three other rows like this, making four rows of nine boxes each.
   Height of triangle = 3 cm
   Base of triangle = 4 cm
   4 rows high = 12 cm
   9 containers in a row
   5 triangles across bottom = 20 cm

   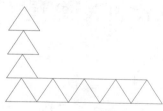

   b) 36 c) 108

7 Link It Together

1. a) Answers will vary depending on the beads selected.
   b) Favourites = 1.51 cm³, Characteristics = 3.94 cm³, Hobbies = 0.97 cm³, Goals = 0.94 cm³
   c) Answers will vary depending on design.

7 Vocabulary Link

1. d) orientation
2. f) right prism
3. a) area
4. g) volume
5. c) height
6. e) right cylinder
7. b) base of a prism

8 Get Ready

1. Explanations will vary. Examples:
   a) +3%. An increase is a positive integer.
   b) –20 m; If sea level 1 is 0, below sea level should be a negative integer.
2. a) +$15   b) –$15
3. a) +3   b) –5   c) +3
4. a) –8   b) +4
5. a) +9   b) –14   c) –3   d) +6
6. a) +3   b) –4   c) –8   d) +3
7. a) 37   b) 19   c) 13   d) 15

8.1 Exploring Integer Multiplication

1. a) positive, insert   b) negative, zero
2. a) $(+5) \times (+4)$ b) $(-7) \times (+3)$
   c) $(-3) \times (+5)$ d) $(+2) \times (+3)$
3. a) $(+1) + (+1) + (+1) + (+1)$
   b) $(-6) + (-6) + (-6)$
   c) $(-2) + (-2) + (-2) + (-2) + (-2)$
   d) $(+9) + (+9)$
4. a) $(+3) \times (+3)$ b) $(-5) \times (+2)$
   c) $(-2) \times (-2)$ d) $(-2) \times (+4)$
5. a) +16   b) –12   c) –8   d) +15
6. a) $(+6) \times (+8) = 48$, Serena will earn $48 dollars over 8 weeks.
   b) $(+12) \times (-3) = -36$, The temperature dropped 36 degrees in 12 hours.

8.2 Multiplying Integers

1. number line, negative
2. a) sign   b) positive, 28, 28
   c) negative, –28, –28
3. same, –24
4. a) $(+2) \times (-3)$ b) $(+3) \times (+4)$
5. Number lines may vary. Example:
   a)

   b)

6. a) +42   b) –32   c) –45   d) +110
7. Estimates may vary.
   a) +162   b) –480   c) –708   d) +1764
8. a) –40   b) +5   c) –2   d) +9   e) +7
9. a) $60   b) –$30

8.3 Exploring Integer Division

1. c) $(-10) \div (+2) = -5$
2. a) $(-8) \div (-4) = +2$
3. b) $(+6) \div (+2) = +3$
4. a) +2   b) +5   c) –2   d) +3
5. a) –5, +2   b) +8, –2   c) +2, +3

6. −3, +4

7. a) +2

b) +2

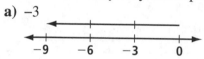

8. a) Each quotient is 1 less than the one before.

   b) −2

9. a) $(+18) \div (+3) = +6$

   b) $(-20) \div (+4) = -5$

10. $(+21) \div (+100)$; 0.21 h or 12.6 min

11. $(+750) \div (+10)$; \$75

8.4 Dividing Integers

1. some, number line

2. numerals, sign   **a)** positive   **b)** negative

3. a) $(+6) \div (+2) = +3$, $(+6) \div (+3) = +2$

   b) $(-8) \div (-2) = +4$, $(-8) \div (-4) = +2$

4. Number lines may vary. Examples:

  a) −3

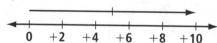

  b) +2

  c) +2

  d) −3

5. a) −11   **b)** −3

6. a) +16   **b)** −1   **c)** −20

7. $(+286) \div (-13) = -22$

8. $(\$15) \div (+5) = +3$ She spent \$3 each day.

9. a) \$15   **b)** 3

10. $(-1972) \div (-35)$, because this quotient is positive and the others are negative

11. 200 m/min

12. 4819 sec or about 80 min

8.5 Applying Integer Operations

1. operation

2. order, operations

3. 1 Brackets; 2 Multiply and divide, from left to right; 3 Add and subtract, from left to right

4. a) −9   **b)** −3   **c)** −12   **d)** −7

5. a) −4   **b)** −31

6. a) 20

   b) $(+12) + (-4) + (+6) + (-10) + (+15) + (+1) = 20$

7. a) 56   **b)** 420   **c)** 243 min

8. a) highest: hours 11 and 14; lowest: hours 8 and 13

   b) Answers may vary. Example:
$$\frac{+2 +1 +1 -3 -1 +4 -1 -2}{8}$$

9. Integer statements may vary.

  a) $(+9) \times (+3) + (-1) + (+1) + (-2) + (-2) + (+3) + (-1) + (+1) = 26$

  b) 36

8 Link It Together

1. $(+100) \times (+290) + (-9) \times (+1000) = +20\,000$, The charity had \$20 000 left.

2. $[(+1000) + (-100)] \div [(+7) + (+1)] = +112.50$, Each person received \$112.50

3. $[(+7) + (+1)] \times (+100) + (-1000) \times (+2) = -1200$

The people at the table won more than they paid for the tickets. The charity lost \$1200 on this table.

8 Vocabulary Link

1. sign rules

2. brackets

3. zero pair

4. order

5. left to right

6. integer

9 Get Ready

1. Descriptions will vary.
   a) letters of the alphabet beginning with *b* and skipping two letters each time
   b) integers beginning with 9 and decreasing by 5 each time

2. Descriptions will vary.
   a)

Figure Number	1	2	3
Number of Squares	4	7	10

   The number of squares begins with 4 and increases by 3 with each new figure.

   b)

Figure Number	1	2	3
Number of Cubes	4	6	8

   The number of cubes begins with 4 and increases by 2 with each new figure.

3. Variables may differ.
   a) $5p$, where p represents the number of pencils in each box
   b) $12d \div 4$, or $3d$, where d represents the number of DVDs in each carton

4. Answers are in italics.

Point	E	C	G	D	A	B	F
x	3	−1	2	3	−1	0	3
y	1	0	−1	2	2	1	0

9.1 Analysing Graphs of Linear Relations

1.

Number of Tickets	1	2	3	4	5
Cost ($)	10	20	30	40	50

2. a, b, e

3. Yes, because the points appear to lie in a straight line.

4. No, because there are no half tickets.

5. a) 3, 2, 9
   b) straight line, linear
   c) 1, 3
   d) Answers are in italics.

Number of Storeys	1	2	3	4	5	10
Total Height (m)	3	6	9	12	15	30

6. a) The points appear to lie in a straight line, showing a linear relation.
   b) 7.5
   c) Answers are in italics.

Volume (L)	Cost ($)
5	7.50
10	15.00
15	22.50
20	30.00

   d) Yes, gasoline is sold in any volume.
   e) $1.50
   f) 25 L = $37.50; 30 L = $45

7. a) Answers may vary. Example: Number of Customers
   b) The points appear to lie in a straight line, showing a linear relation. The graph shows that to move from one point to the next, you go one unit horizontally and four units vertically.
   c) Answers are in italics.

Number of Tables	1	2	3	4	5	6
Maximum Number of Customers	4	8	12	16	20	24

9.2 Patterns in a Table of Values

1. d) ordered pair
2. e) expression
3. a) table of values
4. c) words
5. b) graph
6. the same, the same
7. Graphs may vary. Example:

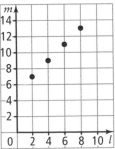

8. a) Explanations may vary. Example: The values increase by the same amount each time.

9. a)

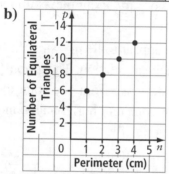

b) 1   **c)** 3   **d)** 3   **e)** $d = 3x$

10. 5

11. a) Answers are in italics.

Number of Triangles	1	2	3	4
Perimeter (cm)	6	8	10	12

b)

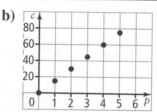

c) Answers may vary. Example: The perimeter of each triangle is twice the number of triangles plus 4.

d) Answers may vary. Example: $P = 2n + 4$, where P = perimeter and n = number of triangles

e) 64 cm

9.3 Linear Relationships

1. a) relation, formula, equation

b) values, reasonable

c) ordered

2. distance, time

3. a) Answers are in italics.

t	v
0	0
1	20
3	60
4	80
5	100

b)

c) Answers will vary. Example: Yes, because the hose could be on for fractions of a minute. Also, if the hose were on for 2 min, 40 L would go through.

4. a) Answers are in italics.

p	0	1	2	3	4	5
c	0	15	30	45	60	75

b)

c) No, because you cannot print partial pages.

5. a) 14   **b)** −11   **c)** 4

6. a) Answers are in italics.

x	−2	−1	0	1	2
y	−7	−3	1	5	9

b) Answers are in italics.

x	−2	−1	0	1	2
y	10	5	0	−5	−10

c) Answers are in italics.

x	−2	−1	0	1	2
y	5	4	3	2	1

7. a) 0, 4   **b)** 1   **c)** 14

9 Link It Together

1.

Time (min)	0	1	2	3
Distance (m)	−60	−40	−20	0

2. a)

b) Scuba Diver's Rate of Ascent

c) Answers will vary. Example: The points appear to lie in a straight line. The graph shows that to move from one point to the next, you go 1 unit horizontally and 20 units vertically.

3. a) Each consecutive value for t changes by 1. Each consecutive value for d changes by 20.

b) $d = 20t - 60$, where d represents distance and t represents time in minutes.

4. No, because a scuba diver cannot swim above the water level.

5. Yes, the data points appear to be in a straight line.

9 Vocabulary Link

1. c) formula
2. f) table of values
3. e) relationship
4. d) linear relation
5. a) equation
6. b) expression
7. g) variable

10 Get Ready

1. a) 19   **b)** 53   **2.** 494 cm²
3. a) $p + 7 = 12$ **b)** $x - 3 = 11$
   c) $4s = 28$ **d)** $k \div 6 = 9$
4. a) 139 cm   **b)** 25 min
5. a) $2n \boxed{+4} = 18$ **b)** $3x \boxed{+5} = 17$
   c) $8y \boxed{-70} = 94$ **d)** $27 = 7q \boxed{+6}$
6. a) $j = 8$ **b)** $t = 3$

10.1 Modelling and Solving One-Step Equations: $ax = b, \dfrac{x}{a} = b$

1. b   **2.** c   **3.** a   **4.** d
5. a) $2r = 8$ **b)** $-3s = 9$ **c)** $\frac{x}{4} = 4$
   d) $-4m = -16$
6. a) $g = -8$ **b)** $p = -9$ **c)** $n = 30$
   d) $b = -21$
7. Models will vary. **a)** $t = -3$ **b)** $b = -8$
8. a) -7 **b)** -8
9. a) $a = -5$ **b)** $k = 9$
10. a) 5   **b)** -4
11. a) no   **b)** no   **c)** yes   **d)** yes
12. a) Equations may vary. Example: $3c = 48$; c is the cost of a child's ticket.
   b) $c = 16$
13. a) $50i = e$ **b)** 50 000 h

10.2 Modelling and Solving Two-Step Equations: $ax + b = c$

1. isolate   **2.** reverse   **3.** substitution
4. negative   **5.** positive
6. a) $3x + 2 = 8, x = 2$
   b) $3x = -6; x = -2$
   c) $2x - 7 = -17; x = -5$
7. a) $\boxed{5+}\, 3x = -7$ **b)** $4r \boxed{-6} = 14$
   c) $13 = -6y \boxed{-11}$ **d)** $-89 = 9t \boxed{-26}$
8. a) $x = 3$ **b)** $p = 4$ **c)** $a = -3$
   d) $d = -3$
9. a) Answers may vary. Example: $4v - 5 = h$, where $4v$ represents 4 times the number of games the Vampires won. Subtract 5 from that to get h, the number of games the Hornets won.   **b)** 6

10. a) no **b)** yes **c)** yes **d)** yes

11. a) $3s + 7 = 40$ **b)** $s = 11$ cm

12. a) $150 + 72p = r$ **b)** $1302 **c)** 25

10.3 Modelling and Solving Two-Step Equations: $\frac{x}{a} + b = c$

1. a) isolate **b)** reverse, add, divide
   c) substituting, value
2. a) $x = 14$ **b)** $a = 8$
3. Models will vary. **a)** $x = 10$
   b) $y = 6$ **c)** $n = -36$ **d)** $c = -49$
4. a) Subtract 2 from each side, then multiply both sides by 6.
   b) Add 6 to each side, then multiply both sides by -3.
   c) Subtract 7 from each side, then multiply both sides by -5.
   d) Add 12 to each side, then multiply both sides by 11.
5. a) $d = -8$ **b)** $n = 32$ **c)** $b = 51$
   d) $p = -13$
6. a) yes **b)** yes **c)** no **d)** yes
7. Equations will vary. Example:
   $\frac{j}{8} + 400 = 475, j = 600$
8. $f = 350$ km/h
9. a) $d = \frac{r}{3} + 137$ **b)** $636 **c)** $370

10.4 Modelling and Solving Two-Step Equations: $a(x + b) = c$

1. isolate **2.** undoing, opposite
3. dividing, distributive
4. answer, sides
5. a) $x = 6$ **b)** $x = 7$ **c)** $x = -3$
   d) $x = -4$
6. a) $t = 7$ **b)** $r = -18$
7. a) $x = 4$ **b)** $s = 146$ **c)** $x = 6$
8. a) Answers will vary. Example:
   $P = 4(l + 4)$ **b)** 60 m
9. a) $3(s + 5) = \frac{180}{2}$ **b)** 25 km/h

10 Link It Together

1. In these answers, d represents depreciation, a represents the age of the car, and c represents the cost of the car.
   a) $d = 1000a$ **b)** $d = a\left(\frac{c}{10}\right)$
   c) $d = (c - 2750)\frac{a}{50}$
2. $3000, $6000, $1035
3. Answers are in italics.

Age of Car (Yr)	Value of Car ($)
0	30 000
1	27 000
2	24 000
5	15 000
8	6000
10	0

10 Vocabulary Link

1. constant
2. distributive
3. reverse
4. equation
5. linear
6. isolate
7. numerical coefficient
8. opposite operations
9. variable

11 Get Ready

1. a) 0.8, 80%   **b)** $\frac{2}{3}$, $66.\overline{6}$%
   c) $0.\overline{36}$ or 0.3636..., 36% or $36.\overline{36}$%
   d) $\frac{1}{3}$, $0.\overline{3}$, or 0.3333...
2. $\frac{1}{3}$, $0.\overline{3}$, $33.\overline{3}$%
3. a)

	1	2	3	4	5	6
A	A, 1	A, 2	A, 3	A, 4	A, 5	A, 6
B	B, 1	B, 2	B, 3	B, 4	B, 5	B, 6

   b) (A, 1), (A, 2), (A, 3), (A, 4), (A, 5), (A, 6), (B, 1), (B, 2), (B, 3), (B, 4), (B, 5), (B, 6)

c) $\frac{4}{12}$ or $\frac{1}{3}$

4. $\frac{2}{3} \times \frac{1}{2} = \frac{1}{3}$

5. $\frac{1}{2}$

11.1 Determining Probabilities Using Tree Diagrams and Tables

1. d) probabilities

2. e) P(A then B)

3. a) probability

4. c) P(A, B)

5. b) tree diagrams

6. Outcomes: (H, 1), (H, 2), (H, 3), (H, 4), (H, 5), (H, 6), (T, 1), (T, 2), (T, 3), (T, 4), (T, 5), (T, 6)

  a) $\frac{1}{12}$ **b)** $\frac{3}{12}$ or $\frac{1}{4}$ **c)** 0

7. a)

	1	2	3	4
3	3, 1	3, 2	3, 3	3, 4
6	6, 1	6, 2	6, 3	6, 4
9	9, 1	9, 2	9, 3	9, 4

  b) $\frac{6}{12}$ or $\frac{1}{2}$

8. a)

Coin Flip	Spin	Outcome
Heads	Dishes	Heads, Dishes
	Garbage	Heads, Garbage
	Vacuum	Heads, Vacuum
	Laundry	Heads, Laundry
Tails	Dishes	Tails, Dishes
	Garbage	Tails, Garbage
	Vacuum	Tails, Vacuum
	Laundry	Tails, Laundry

  b) $\frac{1}{8}$

9. a)

	7	4	1	3	4	9
7	7, 7	7, 4	7, 1	7, 3	7, 4	7, 9
4	4, 7	4, 4	4, 1	4, 3	4, 4	4, 9
1	1, 7	1, 4	1, 1	1, 3	1, 4	1, 9
3	3, 7	3, 4	3, 1	3, 3	3, 4	3, 9
4	4, 7	4, 4	4, 1	4, 3	4, 4	4, 9
9	9, 7	9, 4	9, 1	9, 3	9, 4	9, 9

  b) $\frac{1}{36}$

10. a)

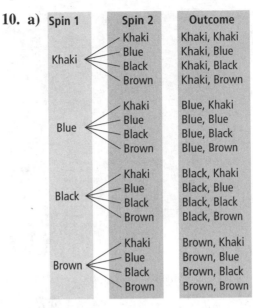

Spin 1	Spin 2	Outcome
Khaki	Khaki	Khaki, Khaki
	Blue	Khaki, Blue
	Black	Khaki, Black
	Brown	Khaki, Brown
Blue	Khaki	Blue, Khaki
	Blue	Blue, Blue
	Black	Blue, Black
	Brown	Blue, Brown
Black	Khaki	Black, Khaki
	Blue	Black, Blue
	Black	Black, Black
	Brown	Black, Brown
Brown	Khaki	Brown, Khaki
	Blue	Brown, Blue
	Black	Brown, Black
	Brown	Brown, Brown

  b) $\frac{4}{16}$ or $\frac{1}{4}$

11.2 Outcomes of Independent Events

1. Order may vary.

  a) tree diagram   **b)** table   **c)** multiplication

2. a)

Yogurt	Fruit	Outcome
Strawberry	Apple	Strawberry, Apple
	Orange	Strawberry, Orange
	Grapes	Strawberry, Grapes
	Banana	Strawberry, Banana
Peach	Apple	Peach, Apple
	Orange	Peach, Orange
	Grapes	Peach, Grapes
	Banana	Peach, Banana
Raspberry	Apple	Raspberry, Apple
	Orange	Raspberry, Orange
	Grapes	Raspberry, Grapes
	Banana	Raspberry, Banana

  b) 12   **c)** $3 \times 4 = 12$

3. a) $4 \times 3 = 12$

  b) Methods may vary. Example:

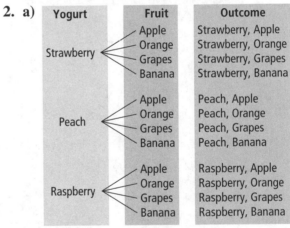

Spinner 1	Spinner 2	Outcome
1	1	1, 1
	2	1, 2
	3	1, 3
2	1	2, 1
	2	2, 2
	3	2, 3
3	1	3, 1
	2	3, 2
	3	3, 3
4	1	4, 1
	2	4, 2
	3	4, 3

4. a)

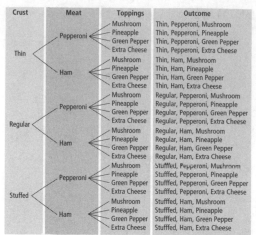

b) $3 \times 2 \times 4 = 24$ **c)** $3 \times 2 \times 3 = 18$

5. a)

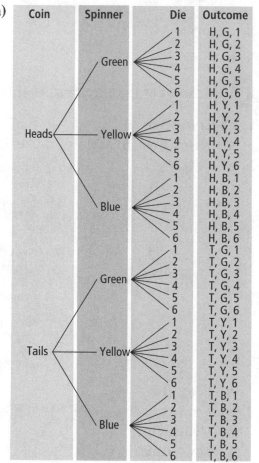

Multiplication, $2 \times 3 \times 6 = 36$

b) 36

6. a) Answers may vary. Example: Andre is taking a trip and has the following options. He can fly or take the train; he can leave on Monday, Tuesday, Wednesday, Thursday, or Friday; and he can choose an economy, regular, or first

class fare. If he selects one option from each category, how many combinations are possible for his trip?

b) Answers may vary, based on question.

11.3 Determining Probabilities Using Fractions

1. a) multiplying, success

b) multiplying, tree diagrams, tables

c) simulation

d) results, experimental

2. a) Methods may vary. Example:

	Purple	Red	Orange
1	1, P	1, R	1, O
2	2, P	2, R	2, O
3	3, P	3, R	3, O
4	4, P	4, R	4, O

b) $\dfrac{1}{12}$

c) $P(4, P) = \dfrac{1}{4} \times \dfrac{1}{3} = \dfrac{1}{12}$

3. a) $P(\text{two gray pencils}) = \dfrac{2}{20}$ or $\dfrac{1}{10}$

b)

Case 1	Case 2	Outcome
B	B	B, B
	B	B, B
	B	B, B
	B	B, B
	G	B, G
B	B	B, B
	B	B, B
	B	B, B
	B	B, B
	G	B, G
G	B	G, B
	B	G, B
	B	G, B
	B	G, B
	G	G, G
G	B	G, B
	B	G, B
	B	G, B
	B	G, B
	G	G ,G

4. a) Answers may vary. Example: I used a four-section spinner marked A, B, C, and D for the classes and pulled the words foyer, library, hallway, gymnasium, cafeteria, and office from a bag. I used a table to record my 20 trials. Experimental probability $P(8C, \text{foyer}) = \dfrac{1}{20}$ or 5%

	F	L	H	G	C	O
8A	✓		✓	✓✓	✓	
8B		✓	✓		✓	
8C	✓		✓	✓	✓✓	✓
8D	✓	✓✓	✓		✓	✓

b) Theoretical probability

$P(8C, \text{foyer}) = \frac{1}{4} \times \frac{1}{6} = \frac{1}{24}$ or 4.17%

c) Answers may vary depending on the results of the simulation. In this example, the theoretrical probability is lower than the experimental probability.

5. a) $P(\text{both shots}) = 15\%$

b) Answers may vary. Example: I considered Greg's statistics and used two spinners. Spinner A represents the first shot. It has 10 equally-sized sectors. I shaded six of them. Spinner B represents the second shot. Spinner B has four equally-sized sectors. I shaded one of these sectors. The shaded sections are the shots he makes. I spun spinner A and then spin spinner B. I repeated this 25 times and recorded the results. Spinner A and spinner B must both land on the shaded part for Greg to make both shots.

Makes Both Shot	Misses One or Both Shots
✓ ✓ ✓ ✓ ✓	✓ ✓ ✓ ✓ ✓ ✓ ✓ ✓ ✓ ✓ ✓ ✓ ✓ ✓ ✓ ✓ ✓ ✓ ✓ ✓

$P(\text{both shots}) = \frac{5}{25} = \frac{1}{5}$ or 20%

c) Answers may vary, depending on the results of the simulation. In this example, the experimental probability is higher than the theoretical probability.

1. a)

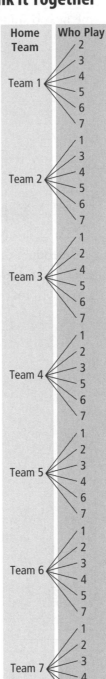

b) 42

c) 7 teams × 6 games each = 42 games

2. a) Answers may vary. Example: I assumed that each team had an equal chance of winning, so I used a two-section spinner

marked Win and Lose. The first 6 spins were for Team 1, the next 6 spins for Team 2, and so on.

	Win	Lose
1	✓ ✓ ✓	✓ ✓ ✓
2	✓ ✓	✓ ✓ ✓ ✓
3	✓ ✓ ✓ ✓	✓ ✓
4	✓ ✓ ✓	✓ ✓ ✓
5	✓ ✓ ✓	✓ ✓ ✓
6	✓ ✓	✓ ✓ ✓ ✓
7	✓	✓ ✓ ✓ ✓ ✓

b) Answers may vary, depending on the results of the simulation. According to the simulation, team 3 will win four games.

11 Vocabulary Link

1. b) favourable outcome
2. f) simulation
3. c) independent
4. e) sample space
5. a) experimental
6. d) probability
7. g) theoretical

```
H  X  F  Q  H  W  F  U  Z  J  E  I  Y  U  U  X  A  I  V  Z
N  F  D  R  X  X  A  B  D  J  X  K  E  J  Y  L  I  N  W  V
C  Y  Q  U  Z  V  V  V  J  J  P  R  N  L  N  W  L  D  W  T
M  M  E  P  Y  S  O  T  M  H  E  G  M  V  G  T  Q  E  F  W
M  F  D  O  F  A  U  R  R  X  R  A  V  Z  W  X  O  P  E  F
I  C  D  D  A  Z  R  Q  P  E  I  B  J  M  X  F  O  E  N  X
Z  W  G  B  Q  M  A  J  V  I  M  T  U  O  O  M  N  N  X  Z
T  H  L  N  F  M  B  N  M  N  E  B  D  I  X  I  L  D  U  Z
K  Q  A  W  L  X  L  Y  D  Z  N  B  K  O  J  U  S  E  A  G
Q  Z  Q  O  T  H  E  O  R  E  T  I  C  A  L  Z  S  N  T  B
Z  D  M  S  Z  B  O  U  V  Z  A  H  O  L  W  E  J  T  I  L
G  B  N  P  P  L  U  M  A  H  L  T  D  N  I  B  E  N  O  K
N  S  W  C  J  Y  T  S  A  M  P  L  E  S  P  A  C  E  N  Q
T  H  C  F  D  E  C  C  Z  P  J  U  F  Z  J  J  C  C  N  K
A  M  W  Z  Z  I  O  S  P  R  O  B  A  B  I  L  I  T  Y  D
W  P  U  Q  J  R  M  U  F  Z  P  U  F  M  Q  T  J  C  T  S
F  M  X  A  C  P  E  X  N  I  N  B  C  V  V  Z  X  R  M  Z
R  V  H  L  A  D  B  I  N  Y  V  X  O  B  O  B  J  G  F  G
```

12 Get Ready

1. **a)** No. Answers may vary. Example: They are not congruent because one of the sides and some of the angles are not equal.
   b) Yes. Answers may vary. Example: They are congruent because all angles and sides correspond.

c) No. Answers may vary. Example: They are not congruent because the circles are different sizes.
d) Yes. Answers may vary. Example: They are congruent because all angles and sides correspond.

2. **a)** Regular. Answers may vary. Example: All sides and all angles are equal.
   b) Regular. Answers may vary. Example: All sides and all angles are equal.
   c) Irregular. Answers may vary. Example: Some of the sides and some of the angles are different.
   d) Irregular. Answers may vary. Example: Some of the sides and some of the angles are different.

3. **a)** $\triangle$THE: $(-4, -2)$, $(-2, -2)$, and $(-2, -4)$. $\triangle$T′H′E′: $(2, -2)$, $(0, -2)$ and $(0, 0)$.
   b) Answers may vary. Example: The direction of rotation is clockwise or counter-clockwise, and the angle of rotation is 180°.

4. **a)**

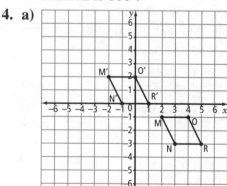

b)

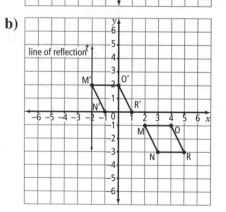

c)

A coordinate grid from −6 to 6 on both axes. Labeled: "line of reflection", points O″, M″, M′, O′, R″, N″, N′, R′ above the x-axis, and M, O, N, R below.

12.1 Exploring Tessellations With Regular and Irregular Polygons

1. c) tessellations
2. d) three, b) regular
3. a) irregular
4. e) vertices
5. a) Yes. Answers may vary. Example: When you put together six triangles, the angle where they meet equals 360°.
   b) Yes. Answers may vary. Example: Where the vertices meet it can equal 360°.
6. Answers may vary. Example:

7. Answers may vary. Examples:

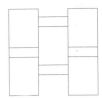

and

8. Answers may vary. Example: This is the tiling pattern on the wall in our bathroom.

9. a) Answers may vary. Example: A shape can tessellate the plane if the sum of the vertices where they meet equals 360°.

b) Answers may vary. Example of shapes that tessellate the plane:

Example of shapes that do not tessellate the plane:

12.2 Constructing Tessellations Using Translations and Reflections

1. tessellations, polygons
2. interior
3. translations, reflections
4. tile, transformed
5. a) parallelogram, triangle
   b) square, triangle
6. Answers may vary. Example:

7. a) Answers may vary. Example:

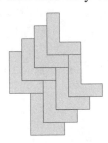

b) Answers may vary, but are limited to any four of T, I, F, H, E, and possibly V.
c) Answers may vary. Example:

8. a) Answers may vary. Example: a reflection and a translation
   b) Answers may vary. Example: multiple translations or a translation and a reflection
9. Answers may vary. Example:

12.3 Constructing Tessellations Using Rotations

1. a) **False** Tessellations can be made with one or more polygons.
   b) **True**
   c) **False** Rotations can be used to create tessellations.
2. a) diamonds   b) hexagons   c) squares
3. a) rotation
   b) rotation or reflection or translation
   c) reflection or rotation or translation
4. parallelograms: reflection; triangles: reflection, rotation and translation
5. Answers may vary. Example:

6. a) Answers may vary. Example:

   b) Answers may vary. Example:

12.4 Creating Escher-Style Tessellations

1. a) Step 3   b) Step 5   c) Step 1
   d) Step 4   e) Step 2
2. a) rotation b) translation
3. a) Answers may vary. Example: The original shape was a square. This was cut to make the shape of a teapot. Parts of the square that were cut off of one side were attached to another part. No part of the square was removed. The resulting teapot design was rotated to make the tessellation.
   b) Answers may vary. Example: The original shape was a square. This was cut to make the shape of a cat's head. The area of the square was maintained. The head was translated left or right and up or down to make the tessellation.
4. a) Answers may vary. Example:

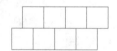

   b) Answers may vary. Example:

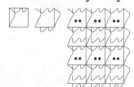

12 Link It Together

1. a) Answers may vary.
   b) Answers may vary. Example:
      Step 1: Start with an 8 cm × 8 cm square heavy piece of paper.
      Step 2: Draw a design on two adjacent edges.
      Step 3: Cut out each design, and then tape it to a piece onto the opposite side. You must attach everything you cut out.

Step 4: Use this as your template and trace your design on the piece of paper. Do not leave any gaps or overlap your paper.

Step 5: Once you have covered the paper, add characteristics to create an animal (be creative), and then colour your design.

c) Answers may vary.

12 Vocabulary Link

1. Escher
2. transformation
3. plane
4. tiling the plane
5. tessellation